BREAKING THROUGH

HOW TO OVERCOME
HOUSEWIVES' DEPRESSION

Marie Morgan

WINSTON PRESS

To the women in the original group
(without whom there would be no story to tell)
for putting the principles into action
and proving that mild depression *can* be overcome

Cover design: Sharon Keegan

The author and publisher gratefully acknowledge permission given by
Prentice-Hall, Inc., Englewood Cliffs, N.J., to reprint previously
published material from John L. Holland, *Making Vocational Choices: A
Theory of Careers,* © 1973, pages 14, 15, 16, 17, 18, 29, and 33.

Scripture texts quoted are taken from *The New English Bible,* copyright
© 1961, 1970 by the Delegates of the Oxford University Press and the
Syndics of the Cambridge University Press. Used by permission.

Library of Congress Catalog Card Number: 82-51157

ISBN: 0-86683-697-7

Printed in the United States of America

5 4 3 2 1

Winston Press
430 Oak Grove
Minneapolis, Minnesota 55403

Contents

1163

Foreword

This book is about one of the most virulent and destructive problems in this latter part of the twentieth century—depression. Today great sums of money are being spent to treat those suffering from the results of depression. While depression itself is not biophysical, it is, nevertheless, a contributing factor in most of our medical problems.

Doctors recognize the toxic effects of wrongly handled stress and unresolved loneliness, of purposelessness and broken relationships. All or any of these may be accompanied by depression. These pathological states are eventually the cause of physical breakdown. Research doctors today are increasingly convinced that emotional, spiritual, and relational problems are at the root of most illness.

In this book Marie Morgan has done pioneer research in the causes, effects, and treatment of depression. Like any good researcher, she has narrowed her field of study. Her own experience with depression was her first laboratory. Then she gathered a group of women around the subject of "Housewives' Depression." Her laboratory grew. Now she lectures and teaches seminars widely, always listening, learning, and expanding her awareness of the subject. Her grassroots research has led to sound psychological, educational, and theological insights.

She is discovering that, while the symptoms of depression may vary greatly between the housewife and the executive, men and women, believers and atheists, the young and the old, the root causes look very much alike. Best of all, she is discovering that depression is treatable, and not just with drugs or expensive counseling.

Much like Alcoholics Anonymous, that phenomenal organization that brought help to the problem drinker at a time when every kind of professional therapy had totally failed, Marie Morgan's small group provides an answer to the depressed. Here they are discovering the power they have to give and are receiving help from one another. The group is the source of affirmation, support, accountability, new self-image, and enthusiasm for living.

It's all here. In reading this book may you discover new resources and strategies—that are as old as the human race. But they still work.

Bruce Larson

How This Book Came to Be Written

Before my first child was born, I heard a friend talk about how unenergetic she felt since she began staying home with her new baby. She had quit an active job and, without really realizing why at the time, was having a great deal of trouble adjusting to the slower pace and isolated world of her tiny apartment. A year later I was in the same situation, again without realizing it. No one warned me that life would be radically different. No one ever talked to me about—I mean really examined—how it would feel to experience this sudden shift in role.

After my second child arrived, I found myself getting much too easily discouraged, then restless, then wondering woefully if life would ever get better. It was several years later, after I had found my way up and out of what I now call "housewives' depression," that I decided to offer a course in my home to share what I'd learned. A reporter got wind of it and did a story. That week I received over fifty phone calls from interested women, each, it seemed, with a thirty-minute story to tell! And I had *already* filled the class by word of mouth! I knew I must be onto a widespread but well-kept secret.

It wasn't until three months later, when I began to notice just how much the lives of the women in the group had changed, that I realized my course must be really effective. I knew then that a book needed to be written to share what we had learned.

I began studying depression in earnest and found that theories of causes abound. And each single-pronged treatment matched its cause. I saw some truth in all of them, from our experience, and I was glad I had instinctively had the sense to weave them together into a more holistic approach (though I'd never heard that term). But I also noticed that the research was on serious, clinical depression. Of course. The women with really serious cases see the professionals, who do the research. Women with the mild depression I had seen so much of rarely realize anything is wrong. So the professionals rarely see them and the researchers rarely write about them. It has been six years since the first housewives' depression group met in my home. Since then I have read that some fifty percent of American women are now working outside the home. But this means the other half are still at home, and for many of them the depression has not gone away.

This book is for all those women who find themselves described in Chapter 1—who may never have realized until now that life *can* be better, brighter, more meaningful, that light and life will soon be breaking through.

Thanks

Writers are seldom at a loss for words—group leaders even less so. But this is the page where it is said . . . thanks!

—to the women in the group that inspired this book: most of all, Carolyn, who convinced me of the need for it, and Nancy, who asked me *every* time she saw me, "How's it coming, Marie?"

—to the Reverend Roberta Hestenes, my first mentor and role model in Christian feminism and ministry

—to Sally Peterson, my mentor in "taking charge"

—to Linda Milavec—one of the most perceptive women I know—who helped me learn to know myself

—to the people who helped me do the writing: Roy Carlisle, the person who first introduced me as "a writer" and who first encouraged me to complete this work; Aaron Milavec, who encouraged me when writing was hard work and no fun at all; Sister Joan Saalfeld, an insightful and patient writing teacher

—to the Reverend Jim Halfaker, the first *man* to understand on a feeling level the need for this book and who encouraged me accordingly

—to the Reverend Lou Taylor, who believed in my writing when I couldn't

—to Doctor Jim Fowler, who introduced me to Winston Press and who taught me that real living has less to do with what we believe than with bringing an active, loving quality to every single day

—to my daughter Christine, who is also a writer, who understands the joy in the seclusion of writing, and who has helped run our home by bringing order out of the chaos

—to my son Peter, whose trust of people and love of life brought me back in touch with the best of what living can be

—to Dean, my husband, who spent innumerable evenings with our children so I could keep writing, listened to endless complaints with a patient smile, and, finally, taught me to finish what I start. Without him there would be no book.

PART ONE

Defining the Problem
and Planning a Strategy

1

What Is "Housewives' Depression"?

"One by one we took our turn backing over the cliff. They'd told us it was less than 150 feet down. Good thing, since our ropes were only 150 feet long! But it looked like a million miles to the bottom. I was scared to death . . . but also very determined to prove to myself I could do it."

Carolyn was describing her recent Outward Bound trip to the ten of us gathered for a one-year reunion of our "How to Overcome Housewives' Depression" group. We listened attentively as she continued. "I knew my ropes were tied securely. I'd tied them myself. I started down, with my feet braced against the rock. As I came to an overhang, I released a little too much rope and I instinctively yelled 'Falling!' The woman at the top caught me short and I suddenly felt foolish. I'd not fallen at all, just panicked a bit. Finally I was down. I've never felt so relieved—or so proud of myself—in my whole life!"

I could see that the women who listened were proud of themselves too. They had each completed their own "wilderness adventure" of sorts in the past year. Twelve months before, they had all meekly assembled in my living room just across town. They did not know each other then. They had dared come only because I, as the leader, had assured each one that she was not alone in her search. They had come to learn how to get rid of what my brochure called "housewives' depression."

I had explained at the very first meeting that a great many women at home experience occasional or chronic depression. A certain percentage become completely unable to function and must see a therapist. But many, many more women have a mild form of depression, which they naturally try to hide from the outside world. Each one feels alone in her discouragement because she sees her friends only when they are at their best, when they venture out of the house. Each one is sure she's the only one who feels that low. I'd emphasized the purpose of the group: to show women they are not alone in feeling mildly depressed; to convince them there is something they themselves can do to change; to teach and reinforce specific methods for getting rid of the depression.

The Signs

What exactly is "housewives' depression"? It is important to understand all that this term implies because many women imagine the gray, tired, listless feeling they have is "just the way life is." These women cannot move toward recovery until they realize life can be better. A look at the personal stories of the women in the original group will illustrate some of the different facets of housewives' depression. Each of their stories gradually unfolded as the weeks moved on.

Carolyn, the woman who recently scaled a 7,000-foot peak and spent two nights alone in the desert, had been a different person four years before. Her daily routine at that time had been to get her young son onto the school bus, then crawl back into bed with the shades drawn until three o'clock. She had had frequent headaches. Her doctor had routinely prescribed Valium to ease her anxiety about life's everyday stressful situations. When her son was in second grade, she suffered a physical collapse; her body just quit coping. She decided then to seek help and began weekly visits to a psychiatrist. After several months of therapy she realized she was getting more help from her weekly neighborhood Bible study and prayer group, where mutual encouragement and support were the practice, than from her psychiatrist. He and she both agreed that what she needed most was the steady support of faithful friends, so she discontinued seeing him. Carolyn decided that the housewives' depression group was a place to solidify gains already made, to strengthen the anti-depression techniques she'd already discovered, and to find added self-confidence and mutual support. Most of all, Carolyn hoped to find some purpose to her life.

Nancy seemed to have more reason than the others to be depressed. She had emphysema from years of heavy smoking. Two years before, when she was thirty-eight, doctors had told her she would spend the rest of her life in a nursing home, lacking the lung capacity to function normally. Nancy had plenty of determination when she started the group, unlike some of the others. She'd just bought her first car, a weary old Datsun, and renewed her driver's license. But she still suffered frequently from depression. Even with her portable oxygen as her constant companion, she couldn't go out of the house on smoggy days. She had to leave meetings if people started to smoke. She did not have the stamina to work full-time and support her two teenagers, so they had to stay in a foster home. She had to fight the temptation to stay in bed and just give up, for she knew her lungs needed the exercise of more activity. Nancy told the group that she came seeking a shred of self-confidence, a taste of how it might feel to be proud of being a woman. She came, as most did, for support to fight for a future.

The two women with new babies shared dilemmas very similar to one another's, despite their ten-year age difference. Lori came to the group overwhelmed with the boredom of being at home after four stimulating years at college. She had had her child at age twenty-three; she loved her baby and wanted to care for him herself, but she had a feeling of being stifled, numb, and tired. Gwen, also a new mother, had been a social worker for eight years before her first baby arrived. "How can it be," she asked the group, "that it takes me five days to do the housework I used to do in one evening when I was working? How can what I've chosen and want to do feel so terrible so often?" She, too, was committed to staying home with her small children, but she was bewildered by the gray, sluggish feeling she had most of the time. She had seen friends farther down the road of depression, so she came to the group hoping to check the problem in its early stages. Both Gwen and Lori were searching for ways to create stimulation and meaning in a world that was driving them crazy.

Jayne, we learned, had two young children and was in her early thirties. She had all the benefits one is "supposed to have" today: a lovely home, well-adjusted children, and a charming, hard-working husband. But she went through periods of extreme discouragement and restlessness. She, too, chose to stay home while her children were young; she loved redecorating the house and working in women's groups. But she felt an undercurrent of unnamed dissatisfaction. Some days she felt life was hopeless and would never change. She once told the group, "Life is so lukewarm. Sometimes I long for some great tragedy in my life just to have something dramatic to react to, something, anything to feel deeply about. Can you believe it?!" She came to the group because she knew enough in her "up" moments to seek new information and group support in tackling the problem, whatever it was.

Sue Ann told us that she had come to realize quite abruptly that she was nearly out of a job, that her services as mother would soon no longer be needed. Her last child was entering his senior year in high school. Her husband had a challenging career that kept him occupied fifty hours a week. He certainly didn't "need her full-time," though they enjoyed a happy marriage. The lack of apparent alternatives was bewildering and depressing her. Sue Ann announced to the group the first week: "I'm forty-three, and I'm here to figure out what I'm going to be when I grow up!"

Jackie was a perfectly groomed blond with a well-scrubbed exuberance and an enormous smile. She surprised us all when she explained, "I had a complete breakdown two years ago . . . simply could not cope with anything. I've been on medication therapy . . . a drug just to help me while I got my bearings. I went off it this month, and I'm here to learn the skills to stay on top of depression without medication."

She explained that some depression is thought to be caused by chemical imbalances in the body. "Doctors are trying to unlock the secrets of this complicated problem. I'm grateful I found a doctor who takes this approach, because nothing else was helping. Now, though, I must eliminate the beginning causes of depression in my world."

Each of these women from the original group (some names and details are changed to protect privacy), like the millions of others who suffer this housewives' "dis-ease," imagined she was the only person in the world to feel as she did. A further look at more of the symptoms may show just how common such experiences can be.

The depressed housewife's mood is often discouraged, sad, bored, or lonely. She may cry easily. She may describe a general sense of hopelessness, whatever her actual situation, as if nothing will ever get better. Her self-image is likely to be poor. While she may have many talents, she cannot recognize them. She feels incompetent or imagines she "does not measure up," or claims she's not very good at anything. In a group, she feels she has nothing to offer. She blames herself for her bad feelings and feels guilty when things go wrong around her, even things over which she has had no control. She may apologize for rain at picnics. Paradoxically, she may feel that forces all around her are working against her and she has no control over her life. She lacks initiative and finds it difficult to begin a task—especially a repetitive one like cleaning or cooking. Physically she is tired much of the time, even though her doctor can find nothing wrong with her. She may have trouble sleeping, or she may want to sleep all the time "to try to get rid of this tired feeling" (or to try to escape the dismal world she faces).

There are at least three stages of life in which housewives' depression occurs quite frequently. All involve a lack of stimulation along with the symptoms already listed. The first stage is one in which a woman, like Lori or Gwen, finds herself at home with one or more small children. She feels demands around the clock, many of them repetitious, such as diaper changing, laundry, and endless toy-picking-up. In the second stage, a woman like Carolyn may find she is depressed when the last child goes off to first grade. The house is suddenly empty and quiet for much of the day. She may have thrived on mothering young children and, as a result, may not have developed satisfying hobbies and activities of her own. Now she finds little to do, once the breakfast dishes are done and the washer is started. When these feelings appear, they are especially bewildering because she has imagined it would be just great having all that time to herself. The third stage often brings foreboding as a woman like Sue Ann anticipates the loss of the entire mothering role and knows of nothing to put in its place. Purpose and meaning suddenly seem to have dropped out of life and she does not know where to turn. She is seldom able to articulate her problem as one of personal identity or lack of a definite purpose. The symptoms of fatigue and boredom accentuate her bogged-down feeling.

Some women may experience mild depression not because of the events of a life stage, but because of a physical limitation like Nancy's. Other women may find vague lingering depression even after they have successfully coped with major depression caused by the death of a parent, child, or spouse. Women who frequently move to new cities are another group who may experience the mild floating type of depression. The "corporate wife syndrome" is a widespread yet little acknowledged form of housewives' depression. There are, no doubt, many other variations on this theme in the stories of countless women who don't know precisely why they feel so low, but know they'd like to feel better.

The Causes

Psychologists, psychiatrists, physicians, sociologists, feminists, social workers, biochemists, and many others have spent years studying depression. Many theories have been investigated and thoroughly documented, and each seems to come to rest on a single cause. Almost invariably "the" cause is discovered within the inquirer's own field of work. Psychotherapists, for example, discern psychological problems: anger, anxiety, loss, or maladjustment to a life situation. Medical researchers point to physical causes, primarily chemical imbalances. Some feminist psychologists regard oppressive circumstances as inherently depressing, while others see depression as the exaggerated extension of traditional societally enforced "feminine" roles.

Clearly there is some truth to all these findings. It is important to note, however, that nearly all the literature on the topic is based on the severely depressed people who have come to professionals for help. Housewives' depression, the kind that seldom reaches the professional's office, has not as frequently come under the researcher's scrutiny. It will be useful for us, nevertheless, to take a closer look at the major theories on depression from the viewpoints of the various disciplines. The following overview is necessarily brief and simplified, but can still give some important insights into housewives' depression and how it might be effectively treated.

Helplessness, in various forms, is considered a major cause of depression. Some researchers find a "feeling of helplessness" to be quite common. Others speak of "learned helplessness" as a mode of acting or reacting. Feminist psychologists today speak of true helplessness or powerlessness. While the feeling-of-helplessness theory focuses on the woman's *feelings* about her world—imagining and acting as if she is powerless to control her environment—the feminists point out that many women are *in fact* powerless in too many aspects of their lives. They have relinquished, or have never had, the ability to make major decisions such as where they will live or what esteem their "job" will carry. In all these cases, a feeling of being trapped is common, and a sense of guilt for feeling trapped "with such a nice home" doubles the burden.

Low self-esteem is sometimes described as a cause of depression, though more frequently it is recognized as a symptom. Either way, an improved self-image is central to any treatment program.

A sense of loss can cause depression. The sense-of-loss theory is most observable in what might be called "event-caused depression": death of a loved one, loss of an important business deal, attainment of a major goal with no future goals in mind, or a sudden change of living locale. Housewives, however, do not usually identify with the sense-of-loss theory because, as Phyllis Chesler, clinical psychologist, points out, women *have never had* (what men get depressed about losing) a positive image of their own future possibilities. This kind of depression is evasive because a woman has trouble pinning down what she feels bad about. It is difficult to identify what isn't there, to trace the outlines of a vacuum.

The Cognitive Therapy approach tries to determine the vague unknowns and sources of confusion in depression. This approach works on the assumption that there is something amiss in the depressed person's understanding and interpreting of her environment. In order to relieve her depression, she must correct her erroneous appraisals of reality. (For example, Suzanne didn't call you, not because she hates you, but simply because she was late getting home.)

Some psychologists have pointed to unexpressed or unresolved anger as a cause of depression. In the last few years, certain aspects of the women's movement have helped women identify and begin to deal with the sources and possible resolutions of their anger. The anger may turn out to be rage and frustration over a lack of alternatives and power choices. In such cases, an active support group can be exceedingly helpful as the woman tries out various avenues of resolution.

Sociologists speak of the isolation the housewife experiences. Her job includes very little contact with other adults beyond perfunctory conversations with clerks or repair people. She is thought to be "loafing" or "gossiping" when she talks to other women. Behavioral psychologists speak of the same cause for depression in terms of a "lack of positive reinforcement" or "unsatisfactory social interactions." A housewife may simply perceive it as "boredom" or "loneliness." My kids call it "not enough warm fuzzies." In any case, solutions called for are external to the depressed woman: create more positive events and relationships.

Psychopharmacologists and some psychiatrists and physicians believe that depression is basically a chemical imbalance in the brain. While there is mounting evidence for this theory, and some very effective drugs are now being used to relieve certain types of depression, little is known about what causes the chemical imbalance itself. Research into the effects of diet and exercise and their possible connection with depression is just beginning. Long-range solutions for when the patient discontinues medication may still require personal and environmental solutions.

While some causes center on the depressed person and "what's wrong with her head," and other causes point to an unsatisfactory environment, some psychotherapists have looked to the sphere of values to find a cause for depression. Logotherapy suggests that having a meaningful purpose for one's life will be the necessary factor in dispelling depression. Integrity therapy operates on the assumption that people are sometimes depressed because they are not living according to whatever values they already hold.

While each of the above causes sheds some light on the subject, life is clearly much more complex than any one single theory can explain. The very fact that there are a multitude of well-researched causes would suggest a multi-cause approach to solutions, even if common sense had not already done so.

What does this book have to add to the discussion of depression, its causes, and treatments? It offers a holistic and usable system for doing away with housewives' depression. It is based on several assumptions:

1. Housewives' depression is caused by a multitude of interwoven factors, not by a single cause demanding a single-thrust treatment. A woman can be fairly successful in combatting mild depression on her own, with the support of friends, by applying a whole cluster of solutions to her situation.

2. Housewives' depression is a mild form of the more severe type of depression that clinical professionals treat. **Women who are completely unable to function, who have contemplated suicide, or who have related alcohol or medical complications should see professionals or specialists and not rely on this self-help book.**

3. Because helplessness or powerlessness is a major factor in housewives' depression, women not only can but must begin to treat their own depression and be mutually supportive of others who are doing so.

This is a self-help book especially designed for peer group use. Experience suggests that while reading this book and doing the assignments alone can be enlightening and helpful, working together on the program in a small support group is infinitely more productive . . . and a lot more fun!

This book offers a "smorgasbord" of practical solutions, a buffet of choices. Each person can take what best suits her individual needs. Unlike a buffet, however, the chapters will be best digested in the order in which they are presented. Later chapters build on the learning acquired in earlier chapters. Part One, for example, gives you the tools to get started. Part Two helps you understand the complexities of depression itself. Part Three challenges you to build permanent changes into your life patterns.

Suggested Assignments

1. If you are reading this book alone (rather than with a group), plan now to set aside a certain time each week to read and do the assignments. You should spend at least a week assimilating and applying the information in each chapter. It takes time to cultivate new patterns of thinking and acting. Give yourself that time.
2. Keep a running list of the symptoms of depression you observe during the coming week. If you were to add your story to Chapter 1, what would you write?
3. Complete the sentence (in writing), "Some things I most want to gain from this book are _____
_____."

   Describe the hopes and goals you are aware of at this time.
4. If you are reading this book with a group, see Part Four for weekly study plans and information on being a good small-group member.

Suggested Readings

James Dobson, *What Wives Wish Their Husbands Knew About Women*. Wheaton, Ill.: Tyndale House, 1975. This gives an overview of the problems women most frequently encounter and serves as a preface to understanding and dealing with mild depression.

Betty Friedan, *The Feminine Mystique*. New York: Dell Publishing, 1974. This is still a classic on the vague dissatisfaction so many women feel.

Mike McGrady, *The Kitchen Sink Papers: My Life as a House-husband*. Garden City, N.Y.: Doubleday, 1975. Here is a delightfully humorous book that demonstrates it's probably one's *role* that depresses, not one's gender. Required reading for anyone who really wants to understand housewives' depression.

2

The Greatest Barrier

"What is the single greatest problem you've had to contend with as you've tried to get rid of depression?" I asked of the women at one of our group meetings.

"Sometimes I feel 'dead in my tracks,'" Carolyn suggested. Lori said she was aware of some strange inertia, as if her body were very heavy and she just didn't want to move it. "I still feel sluggish more mornings than not," Nancy volunteered. As we talked about their feelings, which Sue Ann called "stuckness," it was clear that the women were describing what psychologists call "resistance."

Resistance

Resistance is the single greatest barrier to making depression-fighting programs work. Never underestimate its power to hold you back. It can keep you from calling for a doctor's or dentist's appointment for weeks at a time. It can keep you from visiting a certain friend; you can always find *some* reason not to go. Or resistance can keep you from your education. For several years you've been considering finishing college, yet you never seem to get concrete and specific.

Resistance can take inward or outward forms. Outwardly identifiable symptoms are the easiest to recognize and therefore to deal with. The psychological forms are much more elusive. With the outward form, the person may not feel like getting up off the couch, especially if nothing more interesting than dishes and dirt awaits her. Her limbs often feel lead-filled. A great many women report chronic fatigue. Sue Ann said it was nearly impossible some days to break the magnetic power of the TV set. Gwen was aware of arms and legs passively resisting the mildest of exercise, even though she knew that moving is supposed to wash away the sensation that her bones were made of lead.

Another outward manifestation of resistance is good old procrastination. You tell yourself you do plan to change, to do what you know is good for you, but you'll do it later. "Tomorrow would be a much better day to start the program." This approach makes about as much sense as the man who says, "I'll start lifting weights when I'm stronger." Clearly, the skill comes in practicing, not in waiting for change to happen by itself.

Staying in the house is an indication of resistance; and rationalizing is a tip-off that resistance is operating. Nancy had plenty of good reasons for not going out: fatigue, cost of gas, her hair looking wrong, her belief that people didn't care if she came anyway. She could think of a million excuses to turn back or never get started. All her reasons were true, but she avoided acknowledging the deeper truths, such as a fear of not being liked or accepted. In a more severe form, some women who remain at home actually grow anxious at the thought of going to a meeting and later may develop those same fears about going to their neighborhood supermarket.

The woman who begins to make some progress toward banishing housewives' depression encounters yet another battle with resistance, in a more inward form. She finds it difficult to change her perception of herself and her situation. One of the things depression does is to create a distortion in the part of her mind that evaluates who she is and how well she's doing. She tends to notice the disasters and failures and overlooks the successes. She cannot accept compliments as being true about herself.

Carolyn's initial attitude clearly illustrates this blocking phenomenon. Anyone who meets her quickly sees a close resemblance to Audrey Hepburn: large eyes, classic bone structure, a natural grace, and a ready smile. Carolyn, however, wore her own set of "sunglasses" for many years, which colored and distorted her image of herself. She saw a dowdy woman, an inadequate person who could not cope with life the way she thought she should. As you read this, you may say, "But I *am* dowdy. I'll never be an Audrey Hepburn." The point here is that every woman is special and has her own strong points, abilities, and assets. Your task is to discover whether your "sunglasses" are preventing you from seeing your own best self . . . whether you're getting in your own way.

Sue Ann, at age forty-three, faced the enormous challenge of learning to think of herself as someone other than "mother." Her whole identity, as she was accustomed to perceiving it, had to change; and her whole identity resisted that change.

Hopelessness is a powerful form of distortion and therefore of resistance. It is also a powerful trap. Hopelessness is another way of keeping yourself stuck and at the mercy of events, circumstances, and your low self-esteem. It acts like a strainer or a filter, catching every attempt to initiate a movement or take some step to help yourself.

Sue Ann found herself resisting even looking for an interesting new career. She caught herself thinking, "I'm so old, no one will want to hire me when a cute twenty-two-year-old also applies." Many women face uncooperative husbands who never raise a finger around the house; many women have young children who scatter toys and drawer contents faster than they can be picked up; *everyone* seems to face a money shortage. But a woman sentences herself to guaranteed unhappiness when she decides there is nothing to be done to change her situation for the better. Several women in the original group admitted that they enjoyed wallowing in a certain amount of self-pity from time to time. Self-pity is its own reward and therefore is a particularly insidious way of resisting breaking through to the new you.

When faced with the multitude of small irritations that make up a mildly depressing world, it is easy to play what Eric Berne describes as the "Yes, But" game. Nancy saw that she was playing this game with herself. For example, she would say, "I wish I didn't have to sit around the house so much. It's depressing not having anywhere to go." When someone suggested a meeting or a social event, she always seemed to have a reason to avoid going. "I'd get awfully tired" or "I doubt there'll be anyone there I'd really want to get to know." Every good idea has possible areas of failure, but overcoming this type of resistance means plunging ahead despite them, not allowing the "yes, but" mentality to control.

Another way of identifying your own resistance is to be wary when you find yourself "knowing all the answers." That attitude is typified by one woman who complained, "I've read all the self-help books. Why am I not getting any better?" With a certain amount of informed reading, a person can gain insight and understanding into most of her problems. It's easy to fool yourself for a while, imagining you're on your way. The secret to overcoming this block is to consciously choose one aspect of the information you've mastered and *act* on it . . . *today*.

Overcoming Resistance

Resistance takes many more forms than those just described. And certainly several of these can operate at the same time to subtly undercut your hopes and good intentions. What can be done to overcome resistance? There are three concrete steps you can take: (1) acknowledge the problem, (2) take responsibility, (3) agree to act "as if."

Acknowledging the problem means making a realistic appraisal of your situation. You've probably already realized you're not satisfied with things as they are. It may not seem like much to acknowledge that you feel gray and murky a lot of the time, but pat yourself on the back. Many women think that's "how life is" and never realize things could, indeed should, be better. Acknowledging the specific forms that your own resistance takes can be revealing. One all-too-common form is that of the woman who continually blames her husband or her children, or the serving tasks related to them, for the "fact" that she has no time to herself. Often this blaming is quite unconscious, and so just recognizing that you are doing this is a positive first step toward change.

Taking responsibility for what you plan to change is not only a necessary second step, but an ongoing growth process. You'll find that Chapter 9 deals with the same process in a more detailed way. For now, an honest recognition that you have been and continue to be at least partly responsible for who and where you are will set you on the path toward constructive change. Try using the highly successful Alcoholics Anonymous trick of substituting "I won't" whenever you hear yourself say "I can't." Recognizing your responsibility for getting where you are now provides you with a clearer vision of how much power you have to control your future. Most women vastly underrate the power they have over their own lives.

Sue Ann felt she had no marketable skills as she faced the end of her role of active motherhood. She had put her husband through school and then taken twenty years to raise her children. Her first step was to acknowledge that she *had* made those choices instead of opting for a career. Secondly, she took active responsibility for those choices. She chose, however unknowingly about the future, to take on the roles of helper and mother. Beware, however, of using this need to take responsibility for choices as a weapon against yourself. If you let the process be a judgment against yourself, or let bitterness rule, you set yourself up for more pain. Calm acceptance of the fact that you *are* where you are now is the goal.

The third step (to be introduced here and repeated again and again) is to act "as if" you felt like doing the proposed activity or change. Thousands of successful participants in Alcoholics Anonymous have learned the principle: "It is much easier to act yourself into a new way of feeling than to feel yourself into a new way of acting." Depression is the ultimate but-I-don't-feel-like-it state. You'll never move anywhere if you sit still and wait to feel better. A good starting point is to do the assignment at the end of this chapter that suggests you identify some "as if" areas in your own life.

Acknowledging where you are now, taking responsibility for your behavior, acting as if you feel like doing a task, will help you overcome resistance in its many forms. All these steps are part of the larger process called change. Personal change. Psychological change. Behavioral change. Changing is scary, even when you want it to happen. Worse yet, you too frequently imagine that nothing is changing, that nothing ever will. To better understand the dynamics of how we all change, and to help you see that you are already started, it may be helpful to isolate, perhaps artificially, several of the stages we all go through when we change our behavior and feelings.

How Change Happens

"Why should I feel so bad when I have a lovely home, a kind husband, and two lovely children?" This common question, or one like it, illustrates the *conflict* or *tension* that marks the first awareness that things are not right. When the tension is acknowledged, we begin the second stage of the changing process: *scanning for solutions*. On "high-energy days" our brain may seem to work like a computer, running three shifts in search of an answer. On a "low-energy day" we just mutter and stew and feel frustrated. Sometimes an answer will come while we're in the shower or thinking about something else. The third stage, the *discovery* of a possible solution, we like to call an "ah-ha!" On a low-energy day, resistance may block any action on the discovery; it may even block real recognition that it is an answer. On a high-energy day, the discovery process itself gives impetus to immediate action. You pick up the phone and make a call that very moment.

Once the insight comes, we begin the laborious task of *integrating* the information into our life scheme. Here's where the discomfort reasserts itself. It's a different kind of tension from the "problem" kind, because we have some sense of hope. But it's not often clear how we'll manage to *do* that which is foreseen. It is here, too, that resistance frequently threatens. In Lori's case, she couldn't find any time to be alone and quiet with bustling preschoolers in her care. Her scanning process included the fact that they loved to watch "Sesame Street." The ah-ha came when she realized she didn't *have* to do the dishes and pick up the toys during that hour—she *could* make that her quiet time. The difficulty she had integrating the ah-ha came when she tried to deprogram her personal tape that said, "I can't do anything nice for myself until the house is all picked up."

Another example of the tension/scanning/ah-ha/integrating process: Sue Ann's youngest son was a senior in high school when she identified the restless-mixed-with-useless tension she was feeling. She'd always wished she had finished college, even though she was glad she married instead. The lure of the degree grew stronger, but money was always a problem. The ah-ha came when she discovered her local branch of American Association of University Women and the Soroptimists both gave scholarships to mature women returning to school. The difficult integration that loomed was the multitude of life-rearrangements that would be required to adjust the family to having a serious student in the house instead of a full-time maid, cook, and errand-runner. The initial depression that came from feeling useless subsided when Sue Ann realized she could actually become a college student again. But new depressions arose over the less clean (though still passable) house or the twinges of guilt she felt when she had to remind her husband to pick up his own suit at the cleaners. The change process, then, is continual. New tensions arise as others are resolved.

Why must this changing process be so uncomfortable? Why do we so often try to avoid constructive change in order to maintain our current misery? It's a well-known fact that we resist all kinds of changes: busing children across town, getting a new minister, or accepting a spouse's new hairstyle. Most of the time we would rather keep things the same—safe, predictable, familiar—rather than risk strangeness, newness, and unpredictability. This phenomenon is not surprising when we stop to examine what's going on inside our heads. The patterns we grow accustomed to, however destructive, are familiar. By maintaining them we keep each day smooth.

New patterns pose several apparent threats: (1) We will lack the skills at first to act in the new way (who likes to feel klutzy?); (2) We fear the consequences of the new behavior (we imagine the worst possible, of course!); (3) The new way has no depth, no habits to fall back on when stress requires automatic responses; (4) The very strangeness of the terrain frightens us back into the old familiar path. ("Oh well, I didn't want to go out to lunch with her anyway!") When we analyze the future, we can easily say, "Anything has to be better than the way things are now." But when we begin choosing new paths to counteract the depression, we may get cold feet.

One further note. If it were not for these tensions, these feelings that things should be different, we would get quite bored. In fact, many women get depressed precisely because all the factors in their lives are running so smoothly that there is no change, no challenge. We can welcome the constant flux as opportunity for growth and certainly as relief from deadly boredom.

How long will this changing take? New possibilities dawn on us only as fast as we're ready to put them into effect. If they were to appear any faster than that, we'd not recognize them as applying to us. An assignment at the end of this chapter provides a fascinating life-graph illustration of how much time it may take and how much time you have left to live the results.

Suggested Assignments

1. As you consider making changes in your life, you'll find it helpful to focus on the areas and factors that you may *not* be changing, as a way to acknowledge your firm foundations. Make a list of the things in your life you can be thankful for. List the positive side, for example, of people in your life, physical and social circumstances, your faith, your age, family background, economic situation, neighborhood, education level.

2. If you feel as if your present situation will go on forever, try drawing the following diagram. Draw a line to represent your expected life span. Statistically, you can expect to live to eighty-one. Now mark on the line where you are today:

```
                             38
0                            |                            81
_____
```

If you're thirty-eight, it's slightly to the left of the center. Next, mark off the first eighteen years as time not really your own, but mainly under your parents' influence:

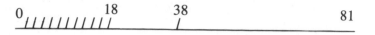

0   18   38   81

Finally, assume it might take as long as a year to put into practice everything suggested in this book. Mark off the distance on the line one year represents. (It's probably no more than a pencil mark's width.) Now you can see graphically how much of the old you has gone before, and how much life as the new you is waiting to be lived.

0 ///////// the old me 38 / the new me 81
/39

3. Identify on paper five parts of your life in which you might begin to act *as if* you felt like doing something. (Example: I'll call a friend and see how she's doing as if I felt like taking that initiative.) Choose one and *do it* this week. Plan when you'll do the other four in subsequent weeks.

Suggested Readings

Eugene Gendlin, *Focusing*. New York: Bantam Books, 1981. A remarkably effective method for getting by our blocks.

John Killinger, *Bread for the Wilderness, Wine for the Journey*. Waco, Tex.: Word, 1976. Not a book specifically on resistance, but one that will delightfully expand your horizons.

1163

3

Getting Started

Two of the most important practices to assist you in beginning and continuing to make personal and situational changes are a journal and a support group. The first is a highly individual activity; the second is obviously an intensely interpersonal process. Together they enhance the two essential parts of each one of us, our private selves and our social selves. Finding permanent ways to overcome housewives' depression will depend on the continual interplay between these two exciting processes.

The Journal

"Some of my problems are so vague, I can't even identify them as tensions, much less scan for possible solutions," Gwen said at the second group meeting. I explained to the women that keeping a journal would be an excellent way to gain clarity in their lives. I ventured to propose that their journal might even be the single greatest tool for personal growth they'd ever discover. I explained, "A journal is a beautiful blank book you talk to without worrying about style. A journal is a place where you record what you're already thinking, not a place where you have to think up something to say." "But I tried to keep a diary when I was young. I'm not consistent enough," Gwen objected. I responded, "A journal has no 'oughts' schedule. You write in it when you think of it, not on somebody else's schedule. There are no guilty feelings for forgetting because whenever you *do* write is the only time you 'should' write."

Journal writing, I pointed out to the women, is simply recording the conversations that go on inside your head all the time anyway. The beauty of the journal is that it remembers what you tell it far better than your brain remembers what you've thought. The act of writing your thoughts on paper drags to the surface thoughts you only glimpse briefly when you merely think them. Sometimes the pen records thoughts you're not really aware you've been thinking, blurry notions and random suggestions about how life is going.

There are at least seven purposes that journal keeping serves: as a record, as a release, as a means of facing problems and formulating clearer thoughts, as a stimulation, as a scan for solutions, and as a way of integrating new ideas into your life.

The first purpose for keeping a journal is simply to record the events and thoughts of your life. You put them down on paper for later scrutiny and reflection.

> Took the car for servicing; walked three blocks to John's parking lot to get his car for the day. Rhododendrons out. Read the mail on the sunny back porch instead of in the messy kitchen: a high point! Macaroni and cheese with romaine salad for dinner.

A second advantage to recording is that the changes and progress in your life become observable and measurable. If you have a particularly bad week, if it actually seems nothing will ever get better, and if you imagine it always has and always will be gray and yucky, you can look to your journal for facts to the contrary. You can go back and read about the day you

> Woke up to the first sunny day in a week. Actually enjoyed the feel of warm dishwater on my hands, sun on my back. Kids were cheerful and ready early for the bus. Wrote three letters to faraway friends. Got a surprise one in the mail. Today it feels good to be alive!

A written record allows you to count the days of disaster and observe that they are actually growing fewer and farther between.

Release is the second purpose for keeping a journal. There is a certain catharsis in just writing about the mess the day was, or talking out on paper the argument or dilemma you faced. You can feel a delightful release of tension, a great sigh of relief when you see the day's hassles out there in front of you on paper.

> The mixer broke today. I'm so tired of all the machines in my life breaking down. Why can't they build things to work? I'm tired of feeling ripped off! The lawn mower isn't even back from the shop yet!! Aagggghhhh!!

Facing inner conflicts, acknowledging feelings, and recognizing dilemmas for what they are comprise the third benefit of journal writing. The tension in the first stage of change can be acknowledged and dealt with in a journal. The difficult job of facing yourself is illustrated by Gwen's description of her early journal-keeping experience:

> When I began, it was mostly a few "poems" about my feelings, and then I began just to write about events of the day and how I felt about them, as well as feelings about my life. I wasn't sure when I began it why I felt the compulsion to write it all down, but it did seem important. I was having a lot of mixed-up, almost contradictory feelings. The journal was one place I could put them all down and confront them myself.

Gwen was able to stay with the problems long enough to recognize what they were and, perhaps more important, what they weren't. A significant part of the difficulty in housewives' depression is that you tend to see problems and dilemmas as larger than they really are. Things loom up as awesome or impossible. You fear there is no way you can get clear of the mess. Transcribing these very real woe-is-me thoughts and feelings, admitting to them, clarifying exactly what they are, is the first step to seeing how to cope with the real dilemmas.

Forming clearer thoughts and intentions is the fourth benefit of journal writing. Jayne related her experience to the group one day.

> Standing at the sink, my head was spinning with what a grouch I'd been with my daughter while she got ready for school that morning. I'd fumed at how she would never let anyone cut her too-long bangs. I caught myself

listing all the reasons I was right, trying to justify harping about it to her. I slowly realized that I really wanted to get everyone off to the day with a cheerful attitude. As I finished the dishes, I had a pretty good list of ways to be positive and encouraging about bangs, lunch boxes, and hurry and finish your breakfast. But I realized that if I simply moved on to the next task, chances were I'd be the same old grouch the next morning. So I sat down for ten minutes with my journal and copied down not only the mental list, but also all the frustrations of the entire situation. I dreamt up a few more creative alternatives as I wrote. I was surprised the next morning to see how all that writing seemed to trigger my memory and prod me into new behavior.

Another advantage and delight to journal writing is the way new thoughts are actually stimulated and freshly formed as the pen moves across the page. As you see one thought taking life on the page, the next one pops up, shouting for recognition. You find, as Jayne did, the list of creative ways to handle early mornings actually grows as you write. Ideas which at the sink were only elusive half-thoughts now come out and in writing become fully developed.

The ah-ha experience can be stimulated by writing in a journal. The ah-ha thoughts seem to come from the back of the brain to the pen, much to the front-brain's surprise. Ah-has also come to mind while you read earlier entries, and you must record these new impressions immediately; they can be as fleeting as they are profound. Ah-has can be sudden insights, inspirations, discoveries, or new ways of seeing old things. You may see patterns emerging that were not visible before. You may, for example, in rereading two months of entries, suddenly realize your worst bouts of depression always come the week before your menstrual period. A more elusive realization, until it jumps out at you, may be that you long for your friends to call you and visit for a while, but you never take the initiative to call them. These examples are mundane; ah-has can be profound philosophical insights as well. The point is, writing stimulates you to see in a flash an obvious solution where before you saw only confusion.

Sixth on the list of journal-keeping benefits is scanning. Your journal provides an excellent medium in which to list possibilities endlessly, for fun or profit. You can create extensive lists of ideas and alternatives. There's no need to censor yourself, no need to be sensible or responsible or realistic. The paper before you is liberating. As details and ramifications emerge, the clarifying process deepens. You can fantasize the possibilities on the horizon, live them through on paper, and see how they feel. You can refer to the lists and scenarios again and again for more careful scrutiny and for further insights.

The seventh benefit—integrating new movements into your life—comes as your thoughts begin to evolve and as writing and expressing yourself becomes easier. You'll then look forward to going back and rereading past entries. Sometimes you'll chuckle at how seemingly insurmountable problems have melted away. Other times you'll be reminded of a resolution you'd forgotten but still care about. Most of all, you'll see progress in your own development. After a few months you'll recognize new capabilities developing for coping with a bout of depression. You'll observe more of the specific factors that have contributed to your feelings, little clues at the very beginning of a down time. And, as you reread and learn from your personal history, you'll realize you're developing a whole arsenal of anti-depression weapons.

At the second group meeting, the women were still hesitant about starting their own journals. Here's the list of ideas I gave them to get started. This list should not limit you but merely stimulate your imagination until you can create your own forms. You could, to begin with, simply keep a brief log of what you do. This is a bare-bones beginning but profitable in its own right. If you feel rushed much of the time, this may suffice. Most women-at-home who are depressed, however, feel they have time on their hands or at least have very flexible schedules. A more detailed running log of how you spend your time, and how you feel about it, can prove helpful. You can then reflect weekly on how you perceive your entries, and you can transcribe those reflections.

A third approach is to reflect on events that occurred before you started your journal. What choices have you made? What sorts of thoughts do you recall having? What have been some of your wishes for your life? When you're in the mood for this historical reflecting, the results can be very revealing.

Write down impressions of conversations you've had that day; reflect on meaningful relationships and why they're important to you. Discuss with yourself why you'd like to alter, improve, or develop certain relationships. "I really enjoyed that brief conversation with Coreen Tuesday. I might like to get to know her better."

As you'll learn in Chapter 6, keeping track of how your body is acting and reacting is an essential part of learning to cope with depression. Record the obvious events like monthly periods, diet and diet fluctuations, illness, special energy highs, exercise and all other physical activities out of the routine, medications, and all stimulants or depressants (including coffee, tea, soda pop, and alcohol) you have taken. The list goes on as your awareness becomes sharpened. You'll learn to observe what your body is up to and what you subject it to. On page 28 you'll see some serendipitous ways to record these body notes. You will find this written record quite helpful when you go to correlate bodily changes with mental happenings.

Record the forces exterior to your body: home, outside events, immediate and faraway environments and how they affect you. Chapter 5 will describe in more detail how you can interpret these observations.

The final area you can record and explore is spiritual reflection: thoughts, meditations, and the ah-has of special wisdom. This section can be among your most meaningful and helpful, depending on your own commitment to reflection and to writing here.

Linda, a young woman who is a clinical pastoral counselor and an artist as well, came to talk to the group about journal keeping. Her profession required extensive insights not only into her patients' lives, but into her own life as well. Linda showed the group some of the more refreshing methods she had developed for her own journal. She sometimes duplicated

	M	T	W	Th	F	Sat.	Sun.
Writing		Clipped 2 more articles for ideas!				Caught up this journal	
Tasks/ House					fixed gutters at last!		
People/ Kids		read to Amy					
Reading	Buy Pathfinders				read late while Alan out of town		
Planning	Meal Planning Done					7AM Goals— Reflection time— felt good!	
Moral Responses				call list for Freeze Campaign group			
New Experiences							go watch Marathon

(vertical note between T and W: OTHER — Sat. weekend w/ Alan)

Exercise

JOGGING—
Mon. ✓
Tues. 15 min.
Wed. - ooops!
Th - new resolve - 20 min
Fri - invited to Linda's health club

Alone Time

Tues—walked thru the Arboretum. Hushed + Luscious

Letters

✓ Denise
✓ Jack
☐ Auntie

Dreams

long one on a bridge scene — see dream section.

Troubling image of wrestling —

Risking

Wrote a letter to my Senator on Tues.- Let him know about his vote on Monday!

Diet

- more carrots as nibble snacks
- more water when I get bored — feels good!

Ooops - Oreos Thursday!

HIGHS AND LOWS

Reflections:

Aha! On the days I have a project or task dear to me, I have no trouble getting out of bed.

a design she was particularly pleased with, keeping a three-ring notebook of the "forms." When inspired, she would draw a new design each day. By all means, create the categories most meaningful to you. One illustration appears on page 28.

Nancy asked if there was a particular sort of notebook she should use for her journal. I suggested the group experiment and report their findings. Jayne found that a three-ring looseleaf best suited her "write anywhere and clip it in later" lifestyle. Carolyn preferred the permanence of the hardbound blank books with the elegant covers. Gwen began decorating a spiral notebook with art museum postcard "masterpieces."

Now a word about secret thoughts. Sue Ann was not sure she ever wanted to start a journal because she worried about other people reading it. Obviously this is a risk. But, like driving on the freeway, most of us feel it's a risk worth taking. I suggested she write a "to whom it may concern" letter on page one, saying something like this:

> If you're reading this without my invitation, you may find things that distress you. That's the risk you take in looking inside another person.
>
> Every person has many untold sides. Most people are afraid to commit themselves to writing, so we never know these sides. I dare because through writing I grow.

I advised the group, "Write what you need to say. Apologize if you must. Hide the book. But *do* dare to write."

As you begin your own journal, remember it's not necessary to write every day. Few of us are that disciplined or organized. It *is* important to write down confusing thoughts, discouraging times and events, new ideas, things you want to preserve, high points and tiny ups that should not be forgotten on the down days. Write from need or joy or release, not from schedule or oughtness. Do not, repeat *do not* get depressed because you missed writing. You'll find the process of writing, if kept as a positive experience, really grows on you. It's like talking to a good friend on the phone, someone who's always home and who always listens. Feel good about the journal you create, the place you write, the growth you experience. It's worth it. You're worth it!

The Support Group

"What has been the most important factor in changing your lives for the better?" I asked the group at the end of our final meeting together. "Meeting weekly as a group made all the difference," Jackie said. "Having real people to relate to," added Lori. Sue Ann suggested, "Reading about answers has been helpful, but it doesn't kick you out the door!" She added, "In our group the key was discussion, support, and the prodding . . . the prodding. We kept each other moving." The response was unanimous: small-group involvement had "made all the difference."

Carolyn highlighted the concept of interdependence and mutual support. "I love the feeling that comes when someone says, 'Oh, I've gone through that, too' or the warmth when someone says she's benefited from what you've just shared, or the boost from learning what makes others happy, depressed, confused, angry, mellow, loved."

Research on women's consciousness-raising groups in the past decade has indicated that a profound level of change becomes possible for a woman when she comes to the realization that she's not the only one who feels a particular way. Much the same dawning of awareness occurs when women in housewives' depression groups realize that many other women feel the very same lows they experience. Once this common sharing of the dilemma is realized, the women become free to move on to new levels of change in their perceptions and behavior patterns. Such realization occurs much faster in a group than it can in isolation. An incident that still seems a bit remarkable to mc was actually a crucial factor in the conception of this book. Hearing one of the "star" women in the community—a forty-four-year-old super-achiever, volunteer-everything, mother-of-three, widely read, willing at the drop of a hat to have you in for a morning of coffee and discussion of the world's problems—admit one day, "Oh, yes, I have days when I'm very depressed" really astonished me. My astounded response was, "You? How can that be possible? You seem to have everything so 'together.'" I began asking other "together-looking" women if they ever got depressed.

A sizable majority said yes. I had discovered a well-kept secret. More important, the very secrecy was blocking solutions. I realized women had to get together if they were to solve this widespread problem. The small group could, with the right study materials, function as a catalyst for insight and growth.

Some women have told me they hesitate to meet with "just women" on a serious basis. They have come to believe that meetings and groups where men are present promise to be much more interesting and "important." Carolyn confided at the fourth meeting, "I've always thought 'ladies' groups' were superficial and stupid. I admit I felt above it all. Getting to know all of you has turned me around. I deeply respect the friendships developing here. Each one of you has a unique gift to give me just by being yourself. I never thought I'd say this, but this group is my favorite place to be each week."

Several of the women nodded, acknowledging Carolyn's feelings. They too had been dubious. They talked together about the image of vacuous or dizzy thinking that the media—especially TV commercials—often give women. Someone admitted it had never even occurred to her to give women a chance; she'd always assumed they would have nothing important to say.

Taking part in a support and growth group is not a luxury; it is a central element in changing and growing, as these women soon learned. There are at least three major reasons why belonging to a support/growth group is central to your success: it helps overcome resistance to change, it counteracts isolation, and it provides models and encouragement.

Resistance requires a whole collection of devices to overcome it. The small group can be one powerful force. There's nothing like another person who cares about you to motivate you to change when you cannot seem to motivate yourself. There's nothing like having to account to the group when your own willpower has failed. The group gently prods you to pursue your goals and ideals. You, in turn, engage in the important ministry of prodding others toward their goals. "They kept me honest!" said Sue Ann, only half in jest.

The small group goes a significant way toward overcoming isolation. Everybody knows housewives are at home all day.

The dilemma is so obvious that it's usually overlooked as a problem. Few people stop to think that the job description requires isolation. If you're with someone else, you "must not be doing your job." You're "loafing" if you are talking to a friend or neighbor. You're "fooling around all day" if you discuss child-raising problems with another woman. You're "gossiping" if you talk at length to the supermarket checker, hairdresser, or neighbor. You're simply annoying if you try to get your tired husband to talk to you when he gets home. To do your best job you should, presumably, stay hard at it with the mop, dishpan, vacuum, and stove. In short, communication with the outside world is considered slouching on the job; the "best" homemakers don't do it.

Consider the double standard: At work men have conferences, brainstorming sessions, and even bull sessions to perform the same functions. They are passing on information on how to cooperate, how to work more effectively, how to encourage each other's efforts, how to make more money for their time or earn more respect for their efforts. The reason these meetings are respected and approved by society (and yours aren't) is that men have always set the rules, and men have said what shall be important. Women can now recognize that they, too, must begin to perform these communication and support functions, set up their own rules for what is important, and take responsibility for how they are going to live.

Women who choose to share and grow together must realize the false wisdom in the American ethic of "rugged individualism." Going it alone may have had some survival value on the frontier, but it's death in the cities and the suburbs. The beauty in true community must be rediscovered and a new urban ethic of interdependence must be established. Women who are at home have both the time and the urgency to create this new ethic.

A third advantage to belonging to a small group is that other members provide both models and encouragement. We all learn on many levels: cognitive (informational), emotional, intuitive, and spiritual. Each individual will be at a different stage of learning on each of these levels. The woman who seems a saint in her spiritual life and serves as an inspiring model for the others may have much to learn from another woman who grasps intellectual content quickly. This second woman may be able to learn a great deal from a third woman who is much more closely in touch with her emotions. How fortunate we are that the sisterhood of mutually teaching and sharing experiences is just now beginning to bloom in our lifetime!

When major behavior patterns are to be changed, the encouragement of the group can be invaluable. Whenever we move into new areas, there is inevitable conflict with the old levels of consciousness, the old patterns. It will, for example, take all the strength the group can offer to support the member who announces to her family that the maid (herself) is no longer working an eighty-hour week. No one likes to lose a maid, and few families appreciate immediately the value of the maid turned part-time artist or musician who takes up residence in the family room instead. It helps immeasurably to have understanding persons available to sustain us through the periods of self-doubt, while new patterns are being established.

Jayne voiced a concern one week that is typical of many women with housewives' depression. She wondered if there was something "wrong" with her . . . why she couldn't seem to "adjust." Together the group discovered, after exploring a long and half-hidden path, that perhaps what was wrong was the *system* they were trying to adjust to. Sue Ann challenged, "Maybe this suburban world we've bought into is unfit for human habitation!" The group began to work on changes to make their immediate personal worlds more satisfying. The group support gave them the courage and know-how to begin to implement the changes.

Two women in the group decided to tackle the inhumane isolation in their neighborhood. They would help each other with housework on a regular basis. They both worked on Mondays at one house, and moved to the other house on Tuesdays. Not only did the work go faster with a friend helping, but they inspired each other to tackle jobs both had been ignoring. Another group member said she would guide day-hikes in the forested trail area east of the city. They arranged specific days-off, planned trail lunches, and several women discovered the exhilaration of a strenuous wilderness walk.

Goals-made-public serve as a powerful motivator. Each person becomes more daring, more imaginative, more prone to optimism. Nancy, who had once been sentenced to a lifetime of bedrest, was challenged by the group to set the goal of one day going skydiving. While all agreed that skydiving might be a bit beyond her that year, Nancy decided to take the helicopter ride at the county fair as a start. That ride became a symbol of the new possibilities she could come to expect of herself.

Coming back to the group when a goal is finally reached solidifies the gains and adds immensely to self-confidence. A good self-image is essential to overcoming depression, and the group's constant evaluation and encouragement work better than hours of individual contemplation to give each woman a strong picture of her strengths.

On a more spiritual level, the group can provide a special quality I call "discernment." That is, as trusted friends get to know you well, they can sometimes help you begin to see things that you could not see alone. They can help analyze your new plans and expectations: Are they realistic, too ambitious and inviting failure, or not daring enough to live up to your true potential? When friends hear you say, "Oh, I couldn't," they ask, "Why not?!"

In conclusion, journal keeping is invaluable in that it provides and enforces quiet time alone. No other activity can replace it. But deep reflective thought, great revelations, and little ah-has do not guarantee new action. Research confirms, however, that nothing promotes action like the prompting and encouragement of friends who care for you and who are in the same predicament. Peer self-help groups are, as Sue Ann testified, "the only way to fly."

Suggested Assignments

1. Enter in your new journal *your story,* which you wrote after Chapter 1.
2. If you're reading this book alone, read Part Four on how to start a support group. Consider finding one friend to help you begin a group to study this book together.

Suggested Readings

Ira Progoff, *At a Journal Workshop*. New York: Dialogue Press, 1975.

Elizabeth O'Connor, *Letters to Scattered Pilgrims*. New York: Harper & Row, 1979. One chapter deals with journal keeping. If you would like to move deeper into this activity, try the many exercises O'Connor suggests. Check your local library and bookstores for more new titles on the subject.

4

Tools for Change

Chapter 1 described housewives' depression. Chapter 2 explained how we resist changing and how change occurs. Chapter 3 described two ongoing change resources, journals and groups. This chapter gets you moving. It outlines several proven ways to take charge of your time, your life, and your ways of doing things. The chapter has several purposes: (1) to help women who are "stuck" get moving in some direction, (2) to identify and begin to dispose of roadblocks to growth and change, (3) to introduce tools and techniques to modify living patterns. This chapter details five methods you can learn to organize and energize your approach to life and to create for yourself a less depressing and more satisfying life.

Problem-Solving

Lori walked into the group during the third week and said, "It's hopeless. I can't get going on any of the things we're supposed to be doing. I trip over toys. I stumble into unfolded laundry. Where do I start? My life seems to be more of a jumble than ever." She had no time, it seemed, to begin to change anything (but babies!). Jayne chimed in. Her life was a swarm of errands and chauffeur jobs. Gwen felt the list of twenty home repair and improvement projects haunting her.

I suggested that we take a few minutes to work through a problem-solving system that would give them a clearer picture of where to start. I explained that we would be breaking their confusing lives down into manageable chunks, small enough for them to deal with one at a time. I could see that this step would be necessary in order to create time and energy for them to work through the rest of the course. I suggested they each

-36-

take ten or so sheets of paper to work with. Then I spelled out on the board the progressive steps to good problem-solving.

1. On your first sheet, list briefly all your problems, whatever comes to mind, and number them. Don't try to anticipate solutions; just list the problems in a few words. Then go back and cross off the ones that are really someone else's responsibility or under their power. For example, "I wish my husband were more cheerful and more interested in my life." Also cross off any which are absurd (even if they're true), like, "I need thirty-six hours each day," or "Do away with mornings." (It's good to write them first to vent the feelings.)

2. For each remaining problem, write a goal on your second sheet, numbering them to correspond to the problem list. Try to do it in the following form:

> On March 8 I will have a moderately well-organized cleaning system that frees me to pursue more enjoyable activities.

You are describing the ideal state as you now imagine it, indicating what things would be like when this problem is solved. Be sure to include an actual date by which you'd like to have it happen. Be as specific as possible so you can tell when you've arrived. It wouldn't be particularly helpful to say, "I want to have a happier relationship with my children." How would you know when that had happened? Instead, you might describe mornings when they leave for school with cheerful outlooks, leaving you feeling "up" instead of drained or discouraged about breakfast-table arguments.

3. Choose the problem that is the most serious, the most annoying, or the one you're most anxious to get at. On a third piece of paper, recopy the problem and the goal statement at the top of the page. Then list in a column, Who, What, When, Where, How much, How often, When start. Note that "How" is *not* one of the questions. An example:

Who:	Me
What:	House, dirt, clutter resolved.
Where:	All rooms except the older children's rooms. Not the garage.

How much:	Pick up enough for friends to drop by without my being embarrassed; clean enough once a week so I don't feel creepy, and spot clean only the rest of the week.
How often:	Weekdays, with one of the five days "off" each week, if special events arise. (Reward for working hard the other four days.) Weekends all control their own contributions to clutter. Clean Friday if entertaining on weekend.
When start:	Next Monday.

4. On a fourth piece of paper, list all the barriers to your goal that you can think of: psychological, interpersonal, economic, legal, social, etc. Again, don't be concerned at this point how you'll overcome all these; just identify them. You are trying to clearly describe and become aware of the scope of the problem. For example:

Psychological barrier: I hate to clean. I'd rather read a magazine and sip tea. I feel annoyed when other people leave their stuff around. If I want to feel clean or have friends in, I have to pick it all up.

Interpersonal barrier: I can't seem to get anyone to quit leaving their stuff around. Yelling doesn't seem to help.

Economic barrier: We can't afford a full-time maid.

Social barrier: People who come to see me may think I'm an awful person if my living room is a disaster area. If they do, I doubt if I can alter their opinions singlehandedly.

Put stars by the barriers you feel you can work on the best. You might, in the above example, eliminate the social barrier at this point.

5. Pick one barrier to start on. On a fifth piece of paper make a list of as many action steps as you can think of. Be creative. List the whimsical, the imaginative, the daring, and the silly. Try to free yourself from the tyranny of listing only the obvious. If you are in a group, you can help each other brainstorm possibilities.

You may decide you will race with yourself to get the picking up done each day, do one major cleaning job, and then reward yourself with a prized activity at 10:30, like reading a magazine with your tea. You will also call a family meeting to discuss the mess problem with everyone else in the house, exploring ways to come to a mutually satisfying solution. The action steps may even include bringing in a cleaning person for three hours on Friday mornings to put the sparkling touches on your week's work and to give everyone a special pride in the place for the weekend. The time and energy released in you may also free you to get an interesting part-time job that would pay for the cleaning services. Alternatively, you may decide to concentrate exclusively on the living room and dining room for the first three weeks until the family's habits are retrained, and to then tackle the less public areas.

Notice that the purpose of breaking the problem down into small steps (the action steps) is to help you avoid feeling the need to solve the whole problem in one day. You can chip away at one area at a time. These small but visible steps will begin to show you some progress. Be glad about what is moving, not depressed about what isn't. Recall the Chinese proverb of the thousand mile journey beginning with a single step.

Here are some additional things to remember about problem-solving: Once you have decided whether you have control over the problem, you must go through a process of accepting the problem. Before you'll be at all effective in solving it, you must *own* it. You can ask yourself these questions (jotting down your answers will help clarify your position): How will working on this fit into my priorities? How serious is the problem? What would the long-term effects be if I ignored it? Will it affect other people? What resources will it use up? Will it cost money to solve? How much of my energy? How much of my energy is used if it's not solved? Will it cause other problems if left unsolved? Will it cause other problems when solved? Remember, there are no right or wrong answers; the purpose is to clarify your own mind and situation.

Look carefully at your options in regard to the problem. You can keep it. You can change its form. Or you can choose to end it. Of course, changing the problem's form may very well end it for you; for example, deciding the children's rooms are *their* problem entirely, and not yours is a creative solution!

Keep trying to find new ways to define your problems, new ways to describe barriers. Get on the track of innovative thinking. We often get stuck because we keep thinking up the same old "solutions" again and again. One woman decided to take everything still on the floor after the school bus left each day and lock it in a box for fourteen days.

For the problems that involve other people, remember to get each person involved in the solution. If it's the laundry room that's driving you crazy, call a family conference. See if you can agree on what the problem actually is—a big step! Then see how many solutions you can brainstorm. Go through the steps for problem-solving listed above. Keep your sense of humor, but beware of the Mom-is-maid solutions. Family members will all assume at first that the problem is entirely yours. You must calmly help them to understand that it's their problem too when they can't find matching socks. Motivation depends heavily on how much of the problem each person owns. Letting everyone in on the decision generates energy and responsibility. We all know how much easier it is to do something we think up than it is to do what someone else tells us to do.

Finally, never underestimate the power of written analysis to motivate you and give you hope and direction. When you discover you are again faced with a life-destroying muddle, go through these problem-solving steps again and start bringing clarity to your life.

Managing Your Time

Lori and Gwen both typified some very common symptoms of depression: feeling that the immediate world is in disarray and feeling hopeless to do anything about it. A short lesson in time management provided the gust of wind that dispelled those gray clouds.

I began the time-management section of the class by asking each woman to analyze precisely what her own time problem was. By asking a series of questions, I outlined three common categories:

1. Do you have *too many things to do*? Is life a constant crush and a rush? Do you try most of the time to be Supermom? Can you objectively examine the standards you hold up for yourself? Do you like to feel that your family could eat off the floor if they chose to? Do you thrive on feeling needed for all the tasks around your home? Is a job superwell done your main source of worthwhile feelings as a person? The issue here is not to judge your standards by certain "oughts," but simply to make you aware of your attitudes. If these are "yes" answers for you, one of your time-management goals will be to learn to set priorities. You'll want to seek clarity in what is truly most important to you and cut down on the running and the frazzling ways of feeling needed.

2. Do you feel you *do not have enough to do that is meaningful* and satisfying? Are you, for example, noticing the children are around less, seem to need you less, and are more and more indifferent to your efforts? If so, you may need to set priorities, but with an eye to building up activities in the areas most meaningful and rewarding to you. This may require a long and interesting discovery process.

3. Do you find you *do not have enough motivation to do the essential tasks* in your life, even though there are plenty of them? Do you find some truth in both of the above paragraphs? Do you feel tired and guilty when you don't do the Supermom things, yet unsatisfied when you do muster the energy? Do you have endless lists of things to do but find only one or two items are crossed off by dinner time and this lack of progress depresses you the next day? Finding out what will motivate you to accomplish that which you want to do and that which you really feel you must do will be part of your goal in time management.

Housewives have one of the most unstructured jobs in the world. To use time wisely and effectively, you must find creative ways to structure your day. Aimlessness and indecision can deepen your depression. On an average morning, for example, you may have a vague, nagging feeling that the laundry, floors, shopping, PTA phoning, and vegetable garden need your attention. You may wish you could get into the new novel you just picked up, but you know if you read it first, you'll feel even worse later. Nevertheless, the prospect of all those semi-distasteful routine tasks gives you a blah feeling, and to console yourself, you pick up *Better Homes and Gardens* and have a second cup of coffee and ignore the breakfast dishes. Later the phone rings and you talk to Helen for half an hour. Patterns like this fritter away the days and create more depression over the undone jobs and the equally unrewarding "leisure" time.

Scheduling and planning can, if done correctly, give you added energy, a zest, and anticipation for your day. But before you begin, consider getting a desk of your own if you don't have one. Begin thinking what kind would best serve your needs and pleasure, for a space all your own will encourage scheduling.

You may devote the first half hour in the morning to planning your day, before anyone else is awake. If this is not your style, consider the first half hour after everyone leaves, or during "Sesame Street" if you have preschoolers, morning nap time if you have a baby. Make it a delightful time to sit and reflect on your true goals and priorities, and to sketch out plans for alternating distasteful tasks with rewarding activities. This might also be your prayer time, a time to consider the value and purpose in the elements of your upcoming day. In any case, try out different times of day until you find a planning time that makes *you* feel best.

How do you know which tasks to start on? There are several categories of tasks that repeatedly appear. One is the important *and* urgent type, for example, income taxes not yet done on April fourteenth or a child who has just broken off a tooth on the sidewalk. There's no debate on how you'll manage your time in either of these instances.

The second category includes tasks important but not urgent. If you had decided to do your income taxes on February fifth, they'd be in this category. Often the goals you set for *yourself* will be important but not urgent. The danger lies in spending time on the categories about to be mentioned, and letting the important goals slip.

Urgent, but not important, tasks make up a huge third category. For example, when you are asked to help with refreshments for the third-grade Columbus Day party, you may not consider it essential to your daughter's educational future, but once you've said yes, you do it within the required deadline.

The fourth category is busy work. Here housewives thrive. You may think up whole lists of projects in order to stimulate an interest in life, such as wallpapering the insides of your closets. Or you may clean the oven once a week, in order to try to feel valuable. Beware of these diversionary tactics. Although worthwhile, they can be great detractors from the truly important goals you'll be establishing. Make distinctions: busy work? or chosen goals?

Once a week you'll want to try to set aside time to reflect on how life, in the long run, is going. Review your journal. Ask yourself how you've moved toward your highest goals. How do you feel about what you did and did not do? Let your journal entry on this reflecting time draw out thoughts and feelings in whatever direction seems natural. The point here is to stay in touch with what is important to you and not let the mundane consume your entire life. The section below on goals and objectives helps you get more specific about where you're heading.

Motivation and Time Management

Keeping interested in the work at hand is one of the primary challenges of the depressed housewife. The women who thrive on homemaking have various ways of talking to themselves, taking pride in their work, or thinking about other things to make repetitious tasks more enjoyable. But for those who are not so moved, more deliberate measures are in order. You must creatively invent ways to make your day more interesting and motivating. One way, which seems to fly in the face of good planning, is to take advantage of your present mood. Let's say you usually clean the bathroom on Friday, but it's Wednesday and you're brushing your teeth when you notice an inordinate amount of toothpaste glopped on the basin. A sudden urge to have the whole sink glistening overwhelms you. (This may be a rare moment!) Instead of being overly tied to your new planning list, you seize the cleanser and sponge and do a ninety-second polishing job on the whole basin and counter. The satisfaction of the clean space is a reward, and the time spent did not seriously disrupt your plans. Naturally, your common sense must govern this "present mood" principle so it doesn't get out of hand. The principle doesn't work when your present mood always wants you to pore over home re-modeling magazines to the exclusion of everything else.

Learn to use your oven timer. Racing with yourself to get everyday jobs done can serve as a great motivator. A bathroom can be cleaned in an hour if you get into the old-toothbrush-scrubbing-the-grout routine. Or it can be done in fifteen minutes to most persons' satisfaction. Set the timer for fourteen minutes and reward yourself with five breaths of fresh air on the porch at the end of the race. You'll feel invigorated for the next task.

If you have a friend with similar low motivation or can pair up in your group, make contracts with each other. Weight Watchers and Alcoholics Anonymous have learned the secret of accountability and support from another person. Call your friend Marge when you've written your day's agenda. Be sure ahead of time that you won't interrupt her quiet time. Tell her what your morning plan is, what you plan to do, and how long it will take. She can do the same, and you can call and congratulate each other at noon, or have a fridge-luck lunch together to celebrate particularly noble cleaning efforts.

As you'll read in Chapter 5, our bodies crave a certain amount of stimulation and change. Newness creates energy in us. You will need, therefore, to plan your day with inventive and interesting tasks interspersed with the duller ones. You might do your jogging through a new neighborhood after you complete the laundry folding. Or promise yourself a phone call to an interesting friend after vacuuming. Again, set the timer for the vacuuming. The added adrenalin stimulated by hustling through this task will yield you more physical energy at the end than plodding through it sluggishly and resentfully.

Be aware of the need for variety and change of pace as you sketch out your daily plan.

Finally, as you set up your plan, program into it some time for true leisure activity. Homemakers are notorious for not giving themselves permission to take vacations. If you're a Supermom, your problem is obvious. If you read a great many magazines, watch TV, and wish you could get motivated to do a little more productive work, you may not realize you too need leisure time. In the latter case, you often feel slightly guilty not doing the vacuuming, so you only marginally enjoy the magazine. Then you feel more sluggish at the end than when you began. Set your schedule up to start the tasks you've decided are crucial to your mental or physical well-being, then as a reward take a truly guilt-free leisure break. It may be a jog over to a friend's for tea and stimulating discussion. It may be a trip to the new coffee, tea, and spices shop or a trip to the library just to browse for fun reading material. The idea is to work hard and then play hard. Let the leisure activity be energizing rather than a subtle energy drain.

Decision-making Helps and Problems

You sit and stare out the window. You can't decide whether it's more important to pull the weeds in the front yard or to re-organize the laundry room for the new system you want to try. Torn by the indecision, you sip coffee and stare at the goals list. Or you take half an hour doing a (productive in other settings) pros and cons list for the two projects. The phone rings and you use the opportunity to talk longer than you might because the indecisive feeling pushes you away from the work. Clearly, to decide on *either one* would have been better than doing neither and wasting most of your morning.

In *How to Get Control of Your Time and Your Life,* Alan Lakein offers a more extensive analysis of how we make decisions. We tend to conform to one or more of the following patterns of decision making:

1. Habit. You run the washer for the required six loads every Friday afternoon because you've always done it that way.

2. Demands of others. "Mom, would you pick me and Fred up after the basketball game so we won't have to walk home in the rain?"

3. Escapism. You imagine how nice it would be to be a good tennis player and be able to really enjoy the game, but you "decide" not to take lessons because you never quite get around to calling to make arrangements. (Actually, unidentified feelings such as a fear of looking foolish may be influencing your choice.)

4. Impulse. You get a burst of energy on Saturday morning and decide it would be fun to have some friends over for dinner.

5. Default. You wait for friends to call you whenever you're bored and feeling lonely.

6. Conscious decision. This is the preferred method most of the time. When planning your week, you assign washing to Monday and Thursday mornings, interspersed with the other cleaning, and fold laundry before lunch as a reward-race. You tell your children the taxi service is now canceled unless there is a genuine emergency. This frees three afternoons a week for activities high on your priority list. One of those days, for six weeks, you set aside for tennis lessons. You discuss week-end plans with your husband every Tuesday over breakfast, and you make your invitation calls that day. Finally, you give yourself a reward after one cleaning task each day by calling one friend you've been meaning to call but haven't.

Parkinson's Law states that work expands to fill the time available for it. This profound if obvious truth emphasizes the need to set oven buzzers or block out specified times for each task on your daily plan. You will have to deal with yourself in some honest fashion if the buzzer goes off and you truly feel you're not finished. You can either reset it for five more minutes or stop and let the rest go for the next time you're on your knees with your head in the shower. The key to dealing with the endless nature of housework is to decide what else you want to get out of life and to stop the mundane when the buzzer sounds.

Procrastination is another time-management problem—one of the worst for some of us. Edwin Bliss suggests three techniques for handling procrastination in his book *Getting Things*

Done. Don't put off trying them. The first method is the "salami" technique; you slice up the job into small pieces. The first step, as soon as you realize you're putting off something big, is to list in writing all the small steps involved in the task. For example, you decide the garage can't be used for storing useful items any longer because it's too full. And next winter there'll be no hope of squeezing the car in. "Cleaning the garage" sounds too hopelessly overwhelming, so you begin your list of salami jobs:

1. Find a clean tablet and pencil.
2. Go out to the garage for ten minutes and list all the things you can see.
3. Bring the list in and enjoy a cup of tea. Snip up the list into piles: Fred's, Joanie's, Ralph's, junk man's, garbage man's, garage sale's, and store-in-the-garage things.
4. Call a family conference to discuss when the others would like to dispose of their things. (You could do this together some weekend, with a celebration barbecue, ending with ice cream sundaes; or each person might wish to attack the job individually, with a two-week junk man-takes-all deadline.)
5. Write on calendar the day(s) "it" is going to be done.
6. Do "it."
7. Call the appropriate people to whisk away the remains.

By breaking down the impossible job into relatively easy and painless steps, which can be done over a series of days, you can usually talk yourself into enough willpower to get moving. Remember, the larger the task looms, the smaller you should make your slices.

The second method for overcoming procrastination is to make a pros and cons list. Draw a line down the middle of a page. List on the left all the reasons you are procrastinating on the job. Be honest with why you are hesitant, what you anticipate will happen if you don't do it, what you fear if you go ahead. On the right, list all the benefits of getting it done, including the specifics of the task and the good feelings (relief, self-praise) you'll experience. The effect should be greater clarity and the motivation to bring yourself all those marvelous benefits.

The third anti-procrastination method is to systematically change your habits. Check your self-talk. Do you catch yourself saying, "That job looks pretty boring, so I'll just ignore it until later when I'm more in the mood"? Sometimes doing the most unpleasant task first is the only way to go. An overdue thank you note, a dentist appointment to be made, an unpleasant phone call all provide a feeling of relief when finally accomplished. Sometimes a tremendous shot of energy can be an added benefit when you realize the job's done. Certainly it's an energy drain if it's postponed.

The feeling of relief and the positive achievement can nurture a new habit. You may come to enjoy those good feelings each day and push yourself to get one unpleasant job done first each morning. Of course, you'll not be doing much you wouldn't have done anyway, just sooner.

Clutter is one of the greatest barriers to decision-making and effective action. It's depressing to feel constantly in a morass of the small items of life. Unfortunately, our awareness of the irritating nature of clutter is not strong enough to motivate us to do away with the mess. The main objection to clutter, other than aesthetic, is that it distracts us from the more important parts of living. If we want to mail a letter but must spend five minutes finding stamps, we may not even get the letter written in the first place. Clutter can be attacked by the salami technique, the problem-solving technique (aimed toward prevention as well), or the tornado technique: just dive in and storm it away. Once again, it's a self-rewarding activity because it feels so good when it's done. Clearing away clutter is one of the most visible ways to bring clarity and energy to your life.

One final note on time management. Your goal in these activities should not necessarily be to become more efficient. Bliss wisely points out that efficiency is an outmoded goal. We should strive instead for effectiveness—deciding Alan Lakein's favorite question: "What is the best use of my time right now?" For example, it may be efficient to clean the silver while you watch the "Today Show." But it may be more effective to wait and clean it when you have a special need for it, rather than having to redo it then. Your time might be better spent with the TV off, working on a higher priority goal.

This section on time management is designed to produce energy in you and clear away some of the fogginess and inertia associated with depression. If you follow the suggestions and plans described, you should have some blocks of time available for discretionary "spending."

Setting Goals and Objectives

Sue Ann was forty-three when she first heard about the concept of setting specific goals for her life. She knew how to plan but never realized she could plan her own life with purpose and direction. Learning to use the concept of goals and objectives freed her for the first time to explore a whole new world of excitement and growth. Similarly, the women in the housewives' group discovered that setting goals and objectives forcefully counteracted the feelings of going in circles, of eternally picking up after other people's lives. They began to glimpse the possibility of having a purpose in life all their own. Carolyn described her discovery: "Energy is actually created inside you by the anticipation of newness." I pointed out to them that *how we perceive* the reality before us fundamentally affects *how we act* toward it.

Modern business has known for years about the methods of planned movement through goals and objectives. Many women's husbands hear about it at management seminars or company training programs, but seldom does the method make its way into the home to help women bring order and purpose to their job. This section is designed to correct that omission by first looking briefly at how to go about drawing up your own goals and objectives, and then by giving specific examples to help you imagine yourself in the process.

The basic procedure is simple: Write down a few *goals* you have for your life. Do several more as five-year goals. Then list some six-month goals. Select one goal, and on a new sheet, begin to list the necessary steps to reach that goal; these are called *objectives*. Depending on the complexity of the activity, your objectives might each have a list of action steps under them. You must then go back and fill in beginning times and completion times, or you'll never get started!

Carolyn, for example, determined during the original housewives' group that she'd always wanted to be a really daring, capable hiker. But on hikes with her husband and son she'd never felt particularly competent in her own right. She heard about Outward Bound and decided, with the group's enthusiastic encouragement, to try to go on the Colorado Outward Bound's Utah desert trip. She chose the ten-day trip the following autumn. Her goals and objectives plan (you can adapt it to your own use) looked like this:

Carolyn _____

January, 19__

MY GOAL IS TO:

apply to and attend a women's course
in the desert next fall

Objective (What needs doing)	Specific Action Steps	When
1. Inquire re: Outward Bound	Write Colo. Outward Bound School	Jan. 10
2. Consult family	Plan evening for discussion	Wk. of Jan. 10
3. Send for and fill out application	Read material	Jan. 10 on
4. Earn money	Look for jobs I do best: secretarial, aide, house cleaning, painting	
Call friends re: job inquiries	Ruth, Marie, Laren	By Mar. 1
5. Save money: $600 by Aug. 1	Make weekly deposits	Mar. 30 on

6. Start exercise program	Exercise 20 min.; jog 2 mi./day	June 15 till D-day!
7. Purchase clothing	Allot money; shop at co-op	Sept. 1
8. Make travel plans	Call airlines	Aug. 1
9. Prepare mentally	Read suggested bks. in cozy place	Mar.-Sept.1 Twice weekly
	Pray in quiet place	Daily
	Call on group for feedback	Weekly
10. Reenter	Unknown at this time	After Oct.

When you write your own goals and objectives, keep in mind that goals must always be accompanied by their requisite objectives. Otherwise you have just transcribed dreams, with no connection to real-life action. Make your goal statements specific by linking them to performance that is measurable. A good statement would be "to be able to run around my four blocks in twelve minutes" or, "to fit into size ten dresses effortlessly."

Being sure your goal is measurable is more important to your success than you may now realize. "To get organized" allows no discernment of how far along you are, or when you'll "arrive." "To draw up a plan every morning" and "to read a book every two weeks as reward for finishing cleaning by 11:00 each day" are measurable goals.

To gain encouragement and support for your new efforts, select a few friends to share your goals with, once you've worked out some objectives and action steps. Do use discrimination here, however, for some of your friends are probably programmed to say, "Why would you want to do *that*?" You don't need that kind of response. Confide in the friend whose typical reaction is "Fantastic! When do you start? How can I help you keep at it?"

As a final step in working up your goal plan, write a short paragraph for each goal. Complete the statement, "When I reach this goal, I will enjoy these benefits: _____
_____." List all the advantages you can think of—psychological, physical, situational, intellectual, social. Or you can write your paragraph in this form: "I'll feel energized and confident, capable and proud of myself when I _____." Rereading your paragraph will give you a boost when you bog down. You'll be highlighting the reasons why the effort is worth it to you. Focusing on rewards combats depression and produces energy for forward movement. Before long you may discover you have more goals than you know what to do with. The fine art of choosing your overall life purpose is discussed in Chapter 10. In the meantime, here's one method for deciding which goals to concentrate on. Take your list of goals and in the margin next to the goals assign one star for each time you answer yes to the following:

_____Is this goal significant to me? Does it matter a lot to me whether I reach it or not?

_____Is this goal urgent? Is this the best time to work on it, or would another time do just as well? Is there a better time to do it? When?

_____Is this goal realistic in my situation right now? (Don't let natural pessimism rule here. This question is simply a reality check to help you decide which goals are most feasible.)

Goals that get three stars could be the ones to start on. Or, you may wish to ask other questions and assign stars on your own criteria. At the end of this chapter you'll find assignments to help you get started with your own goals and objectives.

We turn now to specific methods to get yourself to *do* the things you have determined you want to do, and effective ways to get yourself to *stop* behaviors you no longer like.

Managing Yourself

In Mike McGrady's *The Kitchen Sink Papers* the author-homemaker describes depression as not simply a bad mood, but as "a migraine of a bad mood." He adds, "What distinguished it, also, was my powerlessness against it. If I could have isolated a specific cause, I might have been able to find a specific solution. But there was a lack of definition, an absence of an edge." Our initial response to such a dilemma is to presume that we must be able to define fully what the problem is before we can begin on a solution. With depression this approach is often simply not possible. It's far more effective to simply start somewhere, anywhere. Self-management, as a systematic method, is one excellent starting point. Self-management is a fine way to "isolate a specific solution," even if you cannot "isolate a specific cause."

Do you feel as if most of your actions are decided by the circumstances around you? or perhaps by whim and impulse? or maybe by default or by taking the line of least resistance? The skills of self-management allow you to be more in control of what you do and don't do, and when you do it. You may be familiar with this method under the name "behavior modification." Here we will talk exclusively about how the principles of behavior modification apply to modifying your own behavior, not to how you might modify another's behavior.

The basic principle in self-management is to identify a specific behavior you want to start or stop, select rewards for doing the new thing, act accordingly (keeping records), and then celebrate your new patterns of behavior. Your goal, let us say, is to keep the house picked up, instead of living with the constant clutter. Your first step is to define your goal in a measurable way so you know when you've achieved it. You won't expect to have every stray object off the floor and furniture at every moment, so a more realistic goal needs to be chosen. You might decide to have everything picked up by 9:00 P.M. Or you might prefer to have the public part of the house "party-ready" each Friday by 4:00 P.M. You could define your goal in terms of sections of the house, or times of the day or week, or amount of neatness ("family-comfortable neat" will mean something different than "party-ready neat").

Some writers suggest you keep a chart of how it went so you can mark your improvements. Then choose how you want to alter the situation to achieve your goal. You may decide to steer the children to their friends' houses after school for the first action week of your program. This will give you a head-start and some needed momentum, which having the neighborhood playing in *your* livingroom would not allow. Or, you could alter the situation by hanging new coathooks and book and shoe shelves near the back door and then enlist everyone's cooperation in using them in lieu of the entry hall table. A third alternative (you can use all these and more) would be to integrate this project with your weight-loss goals. Consider stooping down to pick up stray objects as a waist-trimming exercise.

Next, set up rewards for yourself. There will be naturally rewarding consequences to your newly developed behavior. You'll enjoy the neatness for its own sake; you'll enjoy the absence of the uncomfortable sensation the mess used to create; you'll be pleased at not being embarrassed when a neighbor drops in; your husband might notice and applaud you. But you'll probably have to establish specific tangible rewards to begin with until your new habits (and your family's) are well ingrained. You could treat yourself to a lunch out with a friend for every 100 pick-ups. Or, if you're not motivated very well by delayed gratification (and immediate reinforcement *does* work better), establish instant rewards. Read a chapter in your current novel when the picking up is completed. Or call a friend you've wanted to visit. Or invite someone over for 4:00 P.M. and race for that deadline. The most effective reinforcement comes *soon after* the desired behavior, and it comes *frequently*. The more successes you experience, the more likely you'll succeed in your overall program. Give yourself a reward for each room, for example, rather than wait until the entire house is done.

Psychologists suggest you organize social rewards as well. When it comes to housework, though, it's not always easy to get a family to notice, much less compliment you. Don't count on their praise for your measure of success—you'd just be setting yourself up for disappointment. A sympathetic friend might be more reliable for this particular prize.

Notice that this method is not dependent on willpower. Its emphasis involves arranging your environment and your own responses in ways most conducive to your chosen and preferred behaviors. If your goal is related to eating, for example, you can choose the weakest link in the chain between you and the refrigerator in order to curtail snacking when bored. Normally, you identify the restless feeling . . . . You visualize the kitchen . . . . You stop what you're doing and begin walking toward the kitchen . . . . You open the refrigerator door and stare at the contents . . . . Or you walk directly to the cupboard where the cookies are stored. Several options are available to you in planning your self-management program. You could decide to always walk out onto the back porch first, before heading into the kitchen, and do twenty deep knee bends, while breathing deeply. The physiological change brought about by this exercise, the stimulation of more oxygen in your brain, may in itself jar you to the recognition you are not really "hungry." Or you could keep all the cookies in the bottom drawer of the stove behind the waffle iron where you would have to bend and lift to get at them. Or you could decide that you'll only eat cookies while standing in a disagreeable place like the cellar. Use your imagination here. Devise ways to break up your regular patterns of non-thinking action. And give yourself a star on a chart for every time you interrupt the trip to the cookie jar and refrain from munching. You may need to develop another kind of fairly strong and inviting behavior in place of munching for a while. In any case, provide some reward for your refraining behavior.

Here is a list of possible rewards for changed behavior. The emphasis is on free or low-cost items, and ones without calories. Add your own ideas, in writing, as you think of them. Trade lists with the others in your group.

Music

- Put a favorite record on the stereo.
- If you play the piano, treat yourself to a song after one room of picking up.

- Buy a new record for the achievement of a major goal.

Reading

- Read *one* short story in a favorite magazine.
- Start a long-awaited book, one chapter per reward.
- Visit the library and browse in a new section: history of the West, gardening, architecture, new magazines, biographies of women of achievement, stereo records.

Movement

- Do the can-can to a bouncy song on the radio.
- Bend over slowly and see how your spine gradually loosens and your hands slowly get closer to the floor as you consciously relax your neck, shoulder, back, and hip muscles; feel how the blood in your brain further energizes you.
- Walk around the house once, outdoors. See if you can spot ten living creatures (bugs, birds, pets) while you're out there; breathe deeply each time you spot one.

Projects

- Start a craft activity you've been wanting to do: needlepoint, painting, special cooking.
- Complete a project begun long ago: frame some stitchery or an old photograph.
- Design and purchase materials for some object that you'll enjoy building and that will help your goal, such as the back door coat hooks and boot rack.

Outdoor Activities

- Take a cloud-watching walk, or a flower-noticing tour of your neighborhood.
- Collect a list of interesting places in your area that you've not visited: a county museum, a potter's studio, a ballet studio, a neighborhood park across town.
- Borrow a ten-speed bike from a friendly teenager to go riding while he or she is not using it.

Any self-management should work *for* you, as a tool for systematically changing your behavior until it becomes more pleasing to you. Be sure you use the system; don't let the system use you.

Suggested Assignments

1. Identify the three biggest "messes" in your life right now. Choose one that the problem-solving system will clarify, and work through on paper the steps described in the chapter. Have fun watching clarity come from chaos!
2. Which of the three management problem categories is closest to your own situation (page 41)? Start a written list of the time-management tips you intend to begin using in your life. Keep notes on what results you get and which systems work best for you.
3. Choose one goal you would like to accomplish within the next month. Using the outline in this chapter, write down the steps you will use to get there. If you are in a group, share your plan with the others.
4. Select one self-management goal and outline the techniques, reminders, and rewards you'll use to teach yourself the new habit. Share your plans and progress with your group.

Suggested Readings

Alan Lakein, *How to Get Control of Your Time and Your Life*. New York: Signet, 1974. Probably the best time-management book available.

Edwin Bliss, *Getting Things Done: The ABC's of Time Management*. New York: Charles Scribner's Sons, 1976. An excellent handbook.

Edward Dayton, *Tools for Time Management: Christian Perspectives on Managing Priorities*. Grand Rapids:

Zondervan, 1974. Written for business and volunteer organizations but has many good points for women-at-home. See also Chapter 5, "Suggested Readings," for additional time management titles.

PART TWO

Understanding Your Self
and Your World

5

Your Environment

Jayne opened the class discussion one day with a discovery she'd just made. "I used to think there was something wrong with me, that I was awful for not liking cooking and doing dishes more than I did. This week I realized my kitchen faces north, and the walls are grayish brown. My kitchen is dark and depressing!" Jayne had stumbled across an important principle in the battle against depression: Her depression is not entirely in her head. There may well be things in the world *outside* her head that are depressing. This chapter points out some of the environmental factors that can contribute to depression.

Self-help psychology books often concentrate on the ways you can come to better "adjust" to the world around you. One aim of this chapter is to suggest some ways the world can be "adjusted" to you. It makes sense to take a measured appraisal of both yourself *and* your environment. If you were perfectly "adjusted" to your surroundings, you would be molded to fit precisely all the shortcomings of your crazy world. It makes more sense to make some changes in the personal spaces you inhabit and in the time and tasks that await you.

Because feelings of powerlessness are a major cause of housewives' depression, this chapter also emphasizes ways you can have influence and power over your immediate environment. It's not so much your *actual* power over your world as it is your *perceived* inability to affect it that contributes to depression. A depressed person will usually imagine she has a great deal less power than she actually has. The more instances you can create in which you do constructively alter your environment, the more confidence you'll acquire that you have some personal power over your circumstances; that is, you help yourself change your perceptions. Two benefits result from making changes in your environment. First, you get rid of the depressing circumstances or object itself. Second, by creating instances where you *do* have power over part of your world, you combat feelings of powerlessness.

Awareness of Spaces Around You

Jayne discovered the power her kitchen—a most mundane yet necessary part of her world—was having over her daily mood. Most of us are so accustomed to our everyday spaces that we're often unaware of how they are affecting us. To become more aware of your personal spaces, draw a floor plan of your house. A rough sketch will do. Put a star in the room you generally feel most "up" in. Is there a sunny window where you enjoy a cup of tea and a magazine? Do you keep one room warmer than the rest during the winter? Is there a quiet room you can retreat to when the house gets noisy? Locate your own best-feeling space. Second step: Draw a large black dot in the rooms that feel most oppressive. Is your laundry room in the dark, cold basement? Do you try to sew in the always-cluttered "extra room"? Is there a play room that always seems to be a shambles? Have you left your bedroom for last in your fix-up plans and somehow never finished it? And now do you hate to go in there except when the light's off? Identify your own most oppressive spaces, and try to pin down what factors make them that way.

What can you do about these spaces? After you have thoroughly analyzed your personal spaces, with the help of the exercises at the end of this chapter, you can analyze which spaces are changeable and which are not. Jayne decided that natural light in her kitchen was fairly important to her, so she set aside money and had a much larger window installed over her sink. She painted the room yellow and added mirror tiles on the opposite wall. Now the room is noticeably lighter and her attitude noticeably brighter.

When you look at your personal spaces, check the colors of the rooms. How do these colors make you feel? If you live in a rainy climate, a sea-green kitchen may not be helping your outlook, nor will an ice-blue living room. Many new homes are painted throughout in eggshell white. While this scheme reflects a great deal of light (good for countering gloom), it may not provide enough variety and stimulation for your needs. Adding an autumn-gold wall or some carefully placed wallpaper could do wonders for your outlook. Carolyn painted an odd half-wall in her living room mustard yellow and echoed the tone with pillows on her couch. Now there is a ray of sunshine even in the winter, and for the first time she really enjoys being in the room.

If you're not particularly aware of how colors affect you, try tearing pictures (of rooms, textures) out of magazines whenever they please you. Soon you'll begin to see favorite patterns emerging—terra cotta, light tan, fern green. Painting is the cheapest and most dramatic kind of change. Bedspreads and curtains are other one-day possibilities.

Don't begin to think frantic redecorating is *the* answer to depression. Remember, you are beginning to survey a whole network of possible causes for your moods. Altering your immediate environment is just one of many factors you'll want to become aware of and act on.

While you are looking at color, think too of light. How much light does each color reflect? Which direction does each room face? Does your living room let in morning sun, but get gloomy in the afternoon? And when do you allow yourself time on the couch with a good book? Not until 4:00 P.M.? If morning sun energizes you, seek out east-facing rooms for your morning chores, or do your afternoon reading in a west room. Some women have found their moods are affected dramatically by a lack of light. If this is true for you, make the most of sunlight, color, and ample artificial light.

Weather also affects the light that reaches us. Overcast days depress many people, presumably because of the lack of cheery sunlight. But some people suspect that they are particularly sensitive to the lower air pressure that occurs on cloudy days. (Higher pressure occurs on the clear, sunny days.) If this is the case with you, obviously you cannot change the weather. But you can alter the degree to which you let it affect you. A friend in Los Angeles reports, "I don't feel like doing *anything* when I wake up and see it's overcast." But another friend in rainy Seattle says she has decided she's not going to let the weather dictate her life, so she simply ignores the weather on all but the brightest days. On *those* days she celebrates and lets the crisp air energize her to do great things.

Another way to counter gloomy weather and gloomy spaces (you have to go down in the basement to start the washer *sometime!*) is with music. Become aware of which kinds of music cheer you, energize you, delight you. Does Scott Joplin's piano music perk you up when nothing else will? One woman puts on a *Butch Cassidy and The Sundance Kid* tape when she starts to feel gloomy. A Bach violin concerto may be your favorite thing or Barbra Streisand singing "Don't Rain on My Parade!" The important thing is to notice which pieces affect you best and then play them when you need them.

In what other spaces do you spend significant time? Do you garden? Is it a chore or a treat? Sue Ann was vaguely aware that she most loved the fresh smell of the early morning air. Yet she usually put off her gardening until after the other chores were done, leaving her with hot, stale air in late afternoon. When she realized how much it meant to her to enjoy that fresh dew and early sunlight, she changed her schedule around. She gave her whole day an invigorating start by doing thirty minutes of gardening immediately after breakfast.

Do you go shopping as a way of seeking stimulation? How do the shopping areas make you feel? Do you go as a reward for having finished more unpleasant tasks? Or do you prefer to get it over with and return home as quickly as possible? Some women shop out of sheer boredom. Visit any suburban mall at 11:00 A.M. on a Tuesday morning and you'll see the slow pace and blank faces. Merchandisers are aware of this and include art shows, demonstrations, and other events to lure the bored housewife to the shops. The problem arises when these activities fail to deeply satisfy you, and you're still aware of feeling dull when you leave. The lesson here is not necessarily to stop shopping if you're bored but to become more aware of where you spend your time and how those spaces are affecting you. You gain power by consciously choosing what you really want to be doing, instead of letting the environment control you.

Awareness of Time

How do different blocks of time affect you? We know each minute on the clock is equal, yet we've all experienced the seemingly endless time it takes for a late airplane to arrive or the rapid passage of time when guests are due and the toys are not yet out of the living room. What are your feelings about time during your best days? Your worst days? Do you feel more comfortable when you have written a schedule for the day? Or do you thrive on an impulsive routine? If the time-management section of Chapter 4 held special appeal for you, you might want to do a detailed inventory of how your perceptions of time affect your moods.

If lack of stimulation is a major part of your problem, you might try drawing up a specific time chart for the day, as suggested in Chapter 4. It could look like this:

8:00	School bus leaves
	Five minutes to whisk dishes into dishwasher
8:05-8:20	Exercise to one side of a favorite album (to get the juices flowing)
8:20-8:45	Race to complete one major cleaning task
8:45-9:00	Cup of herb tea and write one short letter to a friend
9:00-9:30	Make all necessary phone calls

The trick here is to set the oven timer precisely so it brings you back to an awareness of the passage of time. Breaking up the long stretch of time called "today" can help create a sense of both stimulation and order.

If your problem is one in which time seems to slip by unnoticed and you feel you've accomplished nothing all day, consider some of the "time robbers" listed by Engstrom and Mackenzie in *Managing Your Time*.

1. *Inefficiency*. The worst example is doing the same job twice. Do you wipe off the table while there are still some

dishes on it, only to come back five minutes later to finish the task? Do you sweep some of the obvious crumbs off the kitchen floor, only to return an hour later to clean up the rest? Executives are advised never to handle the same piece of paper twice. The same principle can apply to housewives.

2. *Indecision.* At any given moment at least 247 tasks *could* be done by the average housewife. It's depressing to think of that many undone jobs. While putting them in some priority order can be energizing, belaboring the process can take all morning. It's better to pick something and *do* it, rather than to overwork the decision-making process.

3. *Lack of initiative.* Do you usually wait for circumstances to develop, then react to them? Or do you look for ways to take initiative? You'll be more in control of your time if you do the latter. Chapter 9 is devoted exclusively to the subject of taking charge of your life, but for now let's take a look at a simple example, grocery shopping. Ruth stops by the market whenever she's out of a few things. On Tuesday she may pick up milk, margarine, orange juice, and meat for a couple of nights. She's not home more than two hours when someone finishes off the last of the bread, and she's back down on Wednesday picking up bread and perhaps some onions to go with the meat she bought. If you are already a meal-planner and list-shopper, this example will seem unbelievable. Others of you will recognize just how possible such habits are. Seizing control of this small part of your life can be very energizing, once you develop a simple, workable system.

4. *The mail.* It's easy to make the mail delivery the high point of the day. After all, where else can you find a more likely source of surprise and stimulation? One trouble with preparing too much for this event is that you can waste much time "marking time" until the little truck comes down your street. "I won't start anything now; the mail will be here in twenty minutes." You could race yourself to see if you can get all the sheets into the washer before then, and pat yourself on the back for resisting the temptation to "just glance over this magazine until the mail comes." Another trouble is that you may have a hollow, bleak feeling the rest of the morning if there's nothing but junk mail and bills.

Jackie decided to remedy the "mail call blues" by taking firm action on two fronts. She set aside a definite time each week to write letters to all her out-of-town friends, so she'd get as much mail from them as possible. Then she made picking up the mail from the box a reward for doing her daily fifteen-minute exercise routine. No exercises, no mail.

5. *Misplaced items.* When you're depressed, it's not too exciting to pick up things and put them away. Such endless routine is among the least stimulating parts of keeping house. Yet looking through four rooms and both porches for the broom can be a pretty effective way of never quite getting the kitchen swept. Enjoy the feeling of creating "homes" for the articles that are most frequently missing. Then you'll take pride in putting them there and will feel efficient when you go to use them.

6. *Failure to delegate.* This time robber applies not only to executives, but also to housewives. Unless a woman has children all under the age of two and no husband, there are certainly more household jobs the rest of the family could be doing. Granted, it takes a great deal of energy to get children or husbands started on new tasks, but it's almost always worth the difficult training period. The cheerful attitude you take when you introduce the proposition affects enormously the way they respond to the idea. Consider your home a cooperative community, not a hotel with maid service. Everyone pulls his or her own weight, and you are more the manager than the full-time staff. Books could be written here on the philosophical debate over your own time, on the roles of women today, and on how to reprogram recalcitrant children and spouses. Suffice it to say that if you want more control over your time, consider seriously the issue of delegating work.

A final word on time. Some persons seem to wake up feeling alert and by mid-afternoon they're ready for a nap. They prefer to go to bed early. These are the "morning people." "Night people" have trouble waking up and may hit their energy peak at 10:00 P.M. Plan to take advantage of your higher energy times. You may want to reschedule certain tasks to get them out of the way during a sleepy time, or hustle them through during an alert time. The assignments at the end of this chapter will help you get in touch with other ways in which time affects you and you can affect time. It's another step in getting control of your life.

Awareness of Tasks

It is well known in industry that the most fatiguing jobs are the ones that only partially occupy the worker's attention. Boredom aggravates the fatigue because the worker is just busy enough that she or he cannot concentrate on anything else. Personnel counselors also know that the more the worker's intelligence exceeds the job requirements, the greater the boredom and the greater the likelihood of doing the job poorly. It's not at all surprising, therefore, that housewives experience chronic fatigue, boredom, and eventually depression. The challenge, then, is to spice up some tasks that are draining off your energy and eliminate others.

What tasks need actually be done? Many women who are depressed feel that there are too many household jobs to do, that they'll never catch up, that the waves of responsibility are washing over them and drowning them. Another large group of housewives feel there's not really enough to do. They get all the necessary jobs done by mid-morning and then face an empty and unchallenging day. Someone has suggested that these women trade houses with each other twice a week! Before you dismiss this as a joke, you might seriously consider the possibility of switching houses on occasion with a friend "from the other camp." If you don't actually trade houses, you can discuss very honestly what tasks you each feel compelled to do and, more important, why you feel required to do them. Casual housekeepers can help perfectionists relax a little. Meticulous women can help chaotic housekeepers develop a sense of pride in a job well done. Everyone can pick up a few new ideas to make routine jobs a little more interesting.

Another way to get a clearer perspective on household tasks is to spell out in your journal the problem as you perceive it. Have a conversation with yourself to determine what is actually bothering you. Plug in the problem-solving model from Chapter 4 and see what your alternatives are. You could, for example, phrase the problem, "How can I make my necessary tasks more interesting?" Do this with a friend who has a sense of humor and you'll both come up with ideas that will surprise you. Try reading Erma Bombeck to regain perspective on how not to take it all too seriously. Ask your journal, "What *are* my necessary tasks? What is the worst thing that would happen if each one were left undone? What can I do differently? What can I delegate? Will the neighbors blackball me if I don't rake my shag today?"

Use the assignments at the end of this chapter to develop an inventory of your tasks and how they affect your mood. Develop a written plan for how you will take more and more control over your own job description.

Awareness of Energy Levels

What produces internal energy? What kinds of activities and circumstances make a person feel peppy and industrious? What triggers a zestful spirit? I sent the women in the group on a week-long search for their own energy producers. I explained to them that these "energizers" can be divided into two categories: primary energy sources that originate within the person and secondary sources that originate "out there." Some examples of secondary sources that might produce energy, initiative, and the desire to move are: personal appearance, wealth or possessions (a new dress), status or recognition, and tasks you find enjoyable or interesting. These sources all depend on things occurring outside your self, and they are subject to changes beyond your control. Primary energy sources, on the other hand, are internal. You control them within you to a large degree. Some examples might be your thoughts and memories, your skills and how you feel about them, how you perceive things (noticing the sculpture-like quality of the bare walnut tree), fantasy thoughts, all kinds of creativity (from designing a gift to remodeling your house to art or music), and intellectual activity (reading, writing a short story, learning about photosynthesis, solving a puzzle or a life problem).

If you have trouble seeing the distinction between primary and secondary energy sources, ask, "How easily can someone else take this away from me?" Your status might be destroyed instantly if your husband were fired. Possessions can be swept away in a fire in minutes. Your appearance will be altered with age no matter how ambitiously you work to stem the tide. The point is not to feel you must rely exclusively on primary sources, but to be sure you are not totally dependent on secondary sources. In reality we are all influenced by both types, but most of us need to develop consciously more primary energy sources. Be energized by things you have some control over.

Both types of energy have one essential factor in common: newness. Newness means stimulation, and stimulation can help combat depression. Let's look for a moment at what happens when you encounter something new. At first it stirs up some adrenalin in you. It may be as mild as the feeling you get when you see a pleasant, yet not outstanding, painting. Or it might be the wave of feelings that comes with slipping into a really smashing new dress. After a while, though, the feeling grows familiar; the painting seems to fade, and the dress feels old. Eventually boredom sets in. Observe this with children and new toys: fascination . . . pleasant amusement . . . boredom, and finally complete unawareness of the toy.

Our economy is geared to this satiation reaction. The clothing industry would not be one tenth what it is without the continual craving for something new and exciting. Car fashions change too every year, though few cars are truly worn out in that short time. The examples are endless. Housewives are particularly susceptible to the persuasion of those industries that sell newness because it's a housewife's *job* to buy things. In some circles, your success as a homemaker is measured in how wisely you buy. In others, how lavishly you buy gets you points. For women who experience depression, the key is to find energy sources in a variety of things besides purchases. The effects of new things are not lasting; the results are not truly satisfying. Buying to get rid of depression is a solution with a false bottom.

I suggest you start a list or card file of all the ways you can think of to experience newness without spending money. When was the last time you stopped to really notice those remarkable rainbows produced on an asphalt parking lot by rain on an oil spot? Have you ever noticed a spiderweb on the camellia bush in a dense fog? Every strand is defined by beaded droplets, strung in even rows. Go back the next morning—it's still there, but it's sagging, like an elegant Austrian shade. Stop in front of the lavish old Victorian house downtown. Imagine the delight the carpenter took as he fashioned all those fanciful details. Housekeeping tasks involve much repetition; see how much variety you can introduce. Then trade lists with a friend.

While you're pausing to watch a spider spin its web, reflect on how a sense of order affects you. Does a clean, sparse room energize you? or leave you feeling sterile? Does a room cluttered with collections cause you to feel homey and cozy? Or does it give you compulsive itches to tuck everything into the nearest cabinets? There are no rights and wrongs here. Simply try to clarify for yourself which kinds of situations energize you and which deflate you. Then alter your personal space accordingly.

How does time act on you as an energy source? If realistically set time limits can energize you, learn to use them to your advantage. The urgency to accomplish things can create energy as you work. As you move more quickly, your body is actually stimulated. It may produce some extra adrenalin as you sense the approaching deadline. Try imagining how much adrenalin would be flowing if you were on a game show, the clock was ticking, and a prize you really wanted was waiting for you. If you can get one tenth that much energy going at home on a Monday morning, you'll be bubbling for the rest of the day!

Rewarding yourself for tasks accomplished can also be a source of energy. When you put to work the behavior modification plans outlined in Chapter 4, you'll experience the lift you get when you complete a task and collect your reward. Finishing is its own reward. Remember to seek out the rewards that don't cost money and aren't fattening. You'll feel better later.

If a sense of accomplishment is to serve as its own reward and therefore to energize you, you'll need to consciously create situations in which that can happen. Most of the results of your homemaking are expected, even taken for granted. Even you yourself probably don't think it's a big deal when you successfully vacuum the rug. To create your own sense of accomplishment, you must divide your jobs into the smallest possible chunks. It's easy to view your work as an endless stretch of drudgery. Your alternative is to choose to perceive it one task at a time. You can then recognize your accomplishment one task at a time. Remember, the more you dwell on the endlessness the lower your energy level drops. Don't imagine for a moment your body isn't listening in on those hopeless thoughts! It's ready to quit on you at the first sign from your brain that it's useless to go on. Instead, anticipate with pleasure the feeling you'll experience when the mirror and the chrome faucets are shining or when the rug has vacuum lines all going in the same direction. These mini-rewards are sources of energy you have the power to create and enjoy.

Until quite recently it was thought that "mountains are for men." It's been assumed that the male of the species should be the one to go off and conquer new worlds, discover new serums, solve new problems. This newness, this discovery process, is a tremendous source of energy—a marvelous depression fighter. Women, meanwhile, have been expected to stay put and mind the home fires. Even today, much lip service is paid to the idea that a woman somehow *should* be satisfied with her familiar house for twenty-four years. But this pattern is no longer satisfying, as the millions of women experiencing depression beside those home fires would indicate. Women, too, need new horizons, mountains to climb, new experiences to encounter. Women are learning that "mountains" can serve as excellent sources of energy, zest for life, and a sense of purpose. A new wave of opportunity is opening up for women to experience the world more fully. Many non-radical, peaceful, home-loving women are learning to shape their personal worlds to conform with their innate talents and gifts. They arc learning to seek out challenges, projects with meaning, activities that deeply satisfy them.

The message that "mountains are for men" will persist for some time, however, perhaps more subtly than before. Women who seriously want to overcome depression will have to actively seek and find ways to exercise their primary energy sources and remold their world. And they will have to learn to support each other in the quest, because unexplored paths are scary and intimidating. Women who want to permanently overcome depression will have to seek their own mountains and climb them.

Suggested Assignments

1. Draw a "mood map" of your house. Make note of the areas you wish to alter by making physical changes. Then note changes you'll make in your living patterns to adapt to the space. If you are not in a group, find one friend who would enjoy doing the same assignment, and compare notes.
2. Keep an hourly list of how you spend your time for a week. Go into just enough detail to get a good picture by the end of five days. The following Monday, look at the results and ask, Where do my major blocks of time correspond to my life goals? Where do they not? If you're not sure what your life goals are, see *Strategy for Living* listed below.
3. List your seven most boring tasks. Get together with a friend, or brainstorm in your group, all the crazy ways you can spice up these tasks. See how imaginative you can be. Consider writing it as an article for your local paper.
4. Make an inventory of your tasks. How does your mood affect doing them? How does doing them affect your mood? Are there logical groupings that produce similar reactions? What creative changes can you make? Brainstorm possibilities with a friend.
5. What secondary sources produce energy for you? What primary sources do? Can you increase this list? What

things do you enjoy doing that you seldom get around to actually doing?

6. Start a list of ways to experience newness without spending money. Challenge five friends to draw up their own lists, then pool them. Invite the friend with the longest list over for lunch as a reward.

7. If you have a "stagnation of initiative" or a "loss of spontaneous motivation," you will need to bring some structure and planning to your situation. Get help from the books below or those listed in Chapter 4 and draw up a weekly plan. Give yourself one or two goals for each day. Ask a friend to help keep you accountable to your plan.

Suggested Readings

Stephanie Winston, *Getting Organized*. New York: Warner Books, Inc., 1979. An excellent handbook for organizing and getting your life into shape.

Edward Dayton and Ted Engstrom, *Strategy for Living: How to Make the Best Use of Your Time and Abilities*. Glendale, Calif.: Regal Books, 1976. A time-management book and then some. Focuses on how to set goals, discover priorities, plan to do them, and live according to your plans.

Ted Engstrom and R. Alec Mackenzie, *Managing Your Time*. Grand Rapids, Mich.: Zondervan, 1967.

Pam Young and Peggy Jones, *Sidetracked Home Executives: From Pigpen to Paradise*. New York: Warner Books, 1981. A usable system for actually getting the hundreds of household tasks done. Also hilarious.

Betty Friedan, *The Feminine Mystique*. New York: Dell Publishing, 1974. See Chapter 10, "Housewifery Expands to Fill the Time Available."

Any book by Erma Bombeck, to help you keep perspective and a sense of humor.

6

Your Body

"For me, the anti-depressant drug was *the* answer," Jackie explained to the housewives' group one day. "I was beyond pulling myself up by my bootstraps—I needed outside help." Jackie related what her doctor had explained to her: Some depression is the result of a chemical imbalance in the brain, and an anti-depression drug can sometimes readjust the balance. Jackie had gone through what some would call a nervous breakdown. She could not cope with even the most basic requirements of homemaking and human relationships. Hospitalization had been required. The anti-depression medication had brought her back to a normal life, and now, two years later, she stopped taking it.

A little background on the biochemistry of the brain will help you understand how it is thought depression and the anti-depressants work. The following discussion is not intended to be a medical text. The material is greatly simplified to give you an overview of the process and effects. You may wish to pursue the information in more detail on your own. (See the suggested reading list at the end of this chapter.) The theme of this chapter is awareness of the physical factors that affect you and your depression. With this understanding, you can begin to take charge of the state of your body. You can learn to make critical choices that affect how you feel and how you live. A sense of powerlessness can be one of the causes of depression; awareness of your body's physical processes can give you more power over your own destiny.

Beware of the dangers of self-diagnosis, however. **If you suspect an illness, or find yourself unable to function in the daily activities of your life, or entertain suicidal feelings, consult a physician or a mental health professional. Do not**

let this book be a substitute for a professional diagnosis and professional care.

The Biochemistry of Depression

Today researchers theorize that the following events occur in the brain of every person. There are something like ten billion neurons, or nerve cells, in the typical human brain. Messages are transmitted from one nerve cell to the next by electrical impulses. Each message has to jump across a gap, called a nerve synapse, to get to the next cell. The "bridge" across the synapse is a body chemical called norepinephrine (NE). This chemical is stored in one cell; when it is needed to transmit a message, it shoots out to provide the bridge to the next cell. It is then taken back up on the first side for storage and later use. The theory suggests that with depression the "recycling system" gets out of balance. Either not enough NE is made available, or it is not taken back properly to its starting point. There are other substances, including monoamine oxidase (MAO) to be mentioned later, which "turn off" the flow of NE, either by blocking its flow or by neutralizing it. Depression can sometimes be caused by either a short supply of active NE or an overabundance of these inhibiting substances. Norepinephrine (NE) is related to arousal and alertness, even euphoria and mania. It is a type of adrenalin—an important point to remember in the section below on exercise.

With this basic outline of the nerve cells and how they work, we can take a closer look at the anti-depressant drugs and how they seem to work.

Drug Therapy

Anti-depressant drugs can bring about remarkable mood changes. People who have suffered from serious depression for years become optimistic, easier to live with, and able to cope with most of life's contingencies. But these drugs are not for everyone; they are not "happy pills." The danger of abuse is always present, just as it is with any medication. Consultation with a physician is an essential first step, if you think your depression warrants consideration for drug therapy. If your family physician does not work with psychotherapeutic drugs, and many are not yet familiar with them, he or she may be able to refer you to a physician or psychiatrist who does.

If you do go to a professional who works extensively with drug therapy, be prepared for the possibility that they'll tell you it's not right for your case. It is true that many cases of clinical depression are best treated by these drugs. If there is a definite chemical imbalance, behavior modification may not go far enough to alter it. Trying to improve your self-image will be helpful but, again, perhaps not sufficient. But all drugs can interfere with the body's own marvelous healing devices. Just as you would not take antibiotics for every mild infection, you would not want to take anti-depressants for every dip in your mood.

One test for distinguishing mild "housewives' depression" from the more serious clinical depression (and remember, you can't accurately diagnose it from a book) is to look at your reaction to stimulating events. If you perk up and really enjoy yourself when friends ask you out for dinner or you see a well-done play, for instance, you are probably not suffering from an all-consuming depression. If you notice your depressed feelings primarily when there's very little happening that really "turns you on," you'll probably want to resort to the other approaches suggested in this book to get at solutions. Drugs won't be your magic cure.

The proponents of chemical treatment for depression have not as yet dealt adequately with the question of what *causes* the chemical imbalance in the first place. Certain research indicates a hereditary link in severe depression. Albert Ellis, Aaron Beck, and others have found, however, that sustained and skillful cognitive therapy can sometimes turn around even the most seriously depressed patients. These results would seem to indicate that thinking itself may trigger the chemical imbalances in the brain. Events, of course, such as the sudden death of a loved one, can also trigger depression. Some people snap out of it after a short time; others suffer unusually prolonged depression. The reasons elude us, but more effective treatments become available all the time. Because drug therapy is not generally recommended for mild depression, and because different people respond differently to the variety of other stimuli, this book presents a multi-pronged approach to solutions.

Anti-depressant drugs apparently work because they alter the chemical balance in the nerve synapses. Some people, upon hearing of these anti-depressants, hope they can take "just a little" to try to cure their milder form of depression. It doesn't work that way. A certain quantity of the drug will bring about the needed chemical balance so the nerve cells can function correctly. Smaller doses, it has been demonstrated, are not able to bring about this change, but they still produce the undesirable side effects, so the patient feels terrible without any therapeutic value. These side effects are numerous. They can include: sedation or drowsiness, jaundice, mild Parkinsonian symptoms, hypotension, dryness of the mouth, dizziness, constipation, tachycardia (rapid heartbeat), palpitations, blurred vision, excessive sweating, and loss of sexual interest.

The side effects usually taper off after the first week or so, though a few may persist as long as the drug is taken, such as the dry mouth or blurred vision. The positive results of the drug require two to four weeks to take effect, so a proper understanding of how the drug works is essential. Some patients, accustomed to commercials in which "relief is just seconds away," get discouraged the first week when they feel all side effects and no results. They quit taking the medication before it has had a chance to act. The patient who understands what to expect can counteract some of the side effects, for example, by taking the dosage at bedtime to bypass the drowsiness problem, and drinking additional water and chewing gum to counteract dry mouth. Though the anti-depressants have been a wonder drug for many people, the pros and cons must be weighed carefully, by both the patient and her physician.

Lithium is a drug that has received much publicity in the last few years as an anti-depressant. It's technically not a drug, but simply a salt, in the form of lithium carbonate. Since the publication of such popular books as *Moodswing,* by Dr. Ronald Fieve, the symptoms and treatment of manic depression are much more widely understood. Depression has been described as following one of two types of cycles. In the first cycle, the person lives at a relatively normal level, with periodic dips into depression (unipolar). The second (bipolar) is the manic-depressive cycle, in which periods of high activity alternate with periods of depression. There are often normal levels of activity in between as well.

Once again, some people hear of this "wonder drug" and hope they might take just a little now and then to alleviate their mild symptoms. Lithium is administered to counteract the severe depression valleys in the manic-depressive patient. It also, however, has the effect of leveling off the peaks of high activity. If the peaks are too "hyperactive," this can be helpful. But frequently the highs are times of great creativity, unusual energy, and highly productive work. Dr. Fieve describes several famous personalities in public life, politics, and entertainment who might well be very ordinary people without the up side of their cycles. As Jill Clayburgh's friend in the film *An Unmarried Woman* said, "I'm glad the depression is gone, but I sure do miss the highs."

The side effects of lithium should also be mentioned. Early side effects that soon go away can include: hand tremors, nausea, vomiting, diarrhea, and dry mouth. Other side effects may persist over a long term: blackouts, stupor, vertigo, ataxia (loss of coordination), fatigue, headache, slurred speech, weight change, and hypotension. It should be noted that the dosage of lithium must be carefully determined, and an overdose can be dangerous or even fatal. As with the other anti-depressants, when the depression symptoms are bad enough, it's worth putting up with lithium's side effects to get rid of depression.

Two overwhelmingly popular drugs should also be mentioned in conjunction with depression. One is obtained by prescription, the other is not.

Valium is the most widely prescribed medicine in the world. It has become the answer to innumerable complaints and the source of some controversy. While millions of people are unquestionably helped by this drug, which exerts a depressing effect on the central nervous system and suppresses anxiety, our warning here is against overreliance on covering up symptoms rather than getting at causes.

Many women who suffer from mild depression find themselves anxious about not accomplishing what they feel they "should" or not being the sort of person they "should" be. The depression is often so vague that they can't describe it to their doctors—the feelings sound "silly." The anxiety symptoms are more tangible, and the result is sometimes a Valium prescription to ease that anxiety.

When the anxiety is overwhelming, Valium can restore a balance long enough to allow the patient to manage her affairs and begin to explore causes and alternatives. The danger is in her imagining that the external and behavioral causes of her depression no longer exist. The symptoms may reoccur when she goes off the drug, if she has not taken steps to attack the causes.

The most common self-prescribed drug (after caffeine) is alcohol. Because alcoholism is an illness requiring more attention and expertise than this book can offer, we will not deal with it here in any detail. For women who are not yet bordering on alcoholism but do find that an occasional drink dulls the pain of depression, it is important to recall the effects of this drug. Alcohol is a "downer," a depressant, and a downer is the last thing a person needs when her system is already depressed. Anything that will slow down reactions, put a damper on perceptions, and take the edge off a person's energy is working against her. Instead answers lie in stimulation, activity, heightened interest, and increased energy. If you rely on alcohol to "cope" with your depression, seek help from professionals and from those who have learned to cope more constructively, such as Alcoholics Anonymous. Temporarily covering up your feelings with chemical depressants will not move you toward the better life you seek.

Hormones and Depression

The effects of hormones on the female psyche have become controversial in the last several years. One segment of the women's movement argues that women are no different from men and that there is no discernible effect on a woman's mood that correlates with her monthly menstrual cycle or other hormonal activity. The problem with this argument is that it gives away its proponents' assumption that men are superior when they suggest that females must be inferior if they are different from men. Different doesn't necessarily mean of less value. The more sensible argument points out that not all women are affected in the same way by hormonal changes. Some women may, indeed, hardly notice the difference in body chemistry throughout the month or at menopause; other women do suffer disruptive physical and psychological symptoms.

In order to understand the possible effects that female hormones may have on depression, we need to review the major hormonal changes that occur in the menstrual cycle. The following diagrams are necessarily simplified. They represent a statistical average. Not all women have twenty-eight day cycles; not all women ovulate on the same day within their cycles.

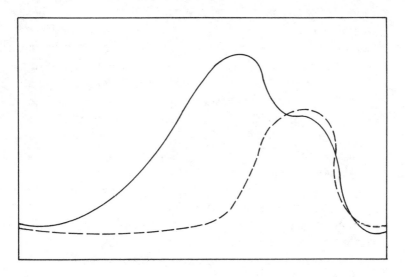

DAY 1   DAY 28
———estrogen   – – – –progesterone

The level of the hormone estrogen is lowest during menstruation. It rises to its highest at mid-cycle, drops off slightly, rises again, then drops off severely just before menstruation begins. Progesterone rises and falls again during the last half of the cycle. It is during this last rapid fall-off that women notice "pre-menstrual tension." This is also when depression is most likely to occur.

Judith Bardwick and her colleagues have researched the mood levels of women to see how hormone levels might affect mood. Their studies of women on sequential and combination oral contraceptives and women not on the pill indicate that mood can be directly related to estrogen and progesterone levels. Mood levels for a woman's normal cycle might be diagrammed over the first chart as follows.

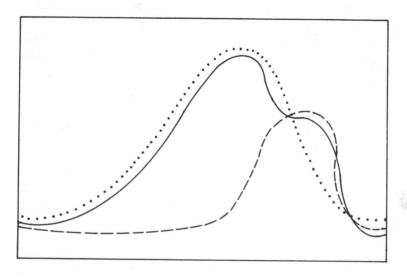

DAY 1   DAY 28

———estrogen   – – – –progesterone   .....mood level

It is thought that the hormones alter the monoamine oxidase (MAO) levels, thereby affecting the level of NE at the nerve synapses. A high level of MAO means too little NE and therefore symptoms of depression. Increased estrogen decreases the MAO level and the depression subsides. Estrogen therapy in menopausal women is known to alleviate some depression. If you are taking an oral contraceptive, or if your mood levels are traceable to your monthly cycle, or if you suspect meno-pausal estrogen decline, check with your doctor about possible alternatives.

If it is helpful to note the possible effects of hormonal levels on moods, it is even more interesting to explore the possible effects of a person's actions and feelings about those actions on subsequent moods. Little is known about how behavior and feelings affect the central nervous system in humans. We do know that hearing a thump upstairs when you are home alone on a dark night will produce both the physiological effect of a racing heart and the emotional feeling of fear or alarm. Studies of rats show an enriched environment both modifies the NE metabolism and increases the size of the nerves' syn-aptic junctions, when compared to rats in impoverished en-vironments and in standard cages. It is risky to leap to con-clusions about humans, but these findings are interesting in light of the fact that many housewives find a stimulating en-vironment *can* alleviate mild depression.

What are you to make of all these findings? How do they relate to your own situation? To determine whether your own moods are related to hormonal activity, you will need to record mood changes in your journal over a number of months. Or, go back and read past entries and see if there is a correlation between low moods and your menstrual cycle.

If you note a time of depression at the point where the hormonal level drops dramatically, you can respond in several ways. One woman simply acknowledged the change. "I know there'll be one day a month where everything will look im-possible and hopeless. I'm irritable, listless, and have no desire to do anything!" Another woman (whose cycle happens to run differently than the chart above) observed from her journal record, "I've had the most discouraged feelings on the twenty-first day of my cycle. No one around me can do anything right." A third woman goes beyond conscious acknowledg-ment and alters her decision-making process. Because she hap-pens to supervise forty employees, she has learned never to fire anyone during her three "down" days. She waits until a few days afterward to see if her decision is indeed warranted.

Some women find that increased exercise during the last half of the cycle will partially ward off the felt effects of the hormone drop-off. Jayne observed, "If I do my twenty-minute run every day, I feel pretty good all month. If I sit around, the feelings of great tragedy hit me like a bomb!"

If you do find a correlation between your hormone level and depression, beware of how you use that knowledge. Don't let your cycle mapping become a trap. If at the first sign of an energy lapse, or a thought of hopelessness, you say, "Oh, estrogen's dropping, no point in trying to do anything for a week," you'll have set yourself up for failure. Instead, let the mapping be a clue for you, or a way of making less mysterious and unexplained the changed feelings you experience. Let the chart say for you, "Here it comes. I'm going to do my very best to do what I'd planned to do before I felt this way."

If other people help keep your mood up, plan more out-of-the-house activities during this down time. Exercise more. Meet an old friend for lunch. Paint a room, if positive, visible accomplishment helps your attitude. Get to bed on time, if you've noticed hopelessness and irritability increase as the late hours wear on. Beware of picking fights with your husband or your children. This may be a time when you are more particular or demanding, or liable to feel less loved and attended to than usual. Like the woman who learned not to fire people, try not to do anything during this time that you'll regret later.

On the positive side, look for ways to use to best advantage the high swings in your mood pattern. Because higher self-esteem and assertiveness are associated with this peak, high-estrogen time, you may want to plan your most daring projects or your biggest accomplishments during these times.

Whatever your particular personal situation, you can make a number of decisions and choices that can positively affect your moods and the ways you manage and respond to them. A proper understanding of how your own body functions is an excellent beginning to a more successfully managed life.

Exercise and Depression

Nancy had never been athletic. Movement other than the basic daily necessities was foreign to her. It simply didn't occur to her to move more than the little she did. After the emphysema hit her, she came to realize that walking might be the key to living a fairly normal life; it would, in fact, be the key to not spending the rest of her life in bed. The value of regular exercise struck her suddenly, like sunlight after a thunderstorm. Most women who are depressed, however, have no such sudden awakening. The gray sluggishness just drags on. Doing exercises is the last thing they *feel* like doing. What they feel most like doing is continuing to sit very still. Or they "treat" themselves by relaxing on the couch for a while, or by escaping the gloom with a nap.

The biological effects (at the neurological level) of exercise on mild depression are not as well researched as we might want. But we can draw some tentative conclusions from what we know about the nerve synapses. Because NE is a type of adrenalin, and because exercise stimulates the production of small amounts of adrenalin in the body, movement can help alleviate depression by "getting the juices flowing." Mountains of articles have appeared recently about the benefits of running and jogging. At the risk of sounding like another bandwagon faddist, I would suggest that a regular exercise program can be a marvelous way to ward off mild depression. Women I have interviewed have frequently reported their gloomy, hopeless moods are immediately dispelled by a twenty-minute walk or run. Regular exercise can provide an overall sense of well-being that may make your depression a thing of the past. Consult one of the many books by running doctors for a carefully planned beginners' program. Look up an Aerobic Dancing class. Or consider bicycling. The scenery changes much faster!

Whatever type of exercise you choose, begin slowly. As your energy level and interest build, you can increase your ambitions. The idea of a regimented forty-minute daily calisthenics program can sound pretty depressing! Choose one of your more energetic days to consider which types of activity most appeal to you, and make note of them in your journal.

The concept of inertia in physics may help you understand what you're up against on your "I don't feel like moving" days. You have probably noticed how hard it is to push a stalled car by hand. It takes all the strain of every muscle at first, but once it's rolling, even on the level, you can maintain the rolling with less effort. The same is true for exercising. Getting up off the couch is the most difficult part. Once you're moving, adding a little exertion is less trouble, and may even begin to feel good. As the "juices" begin to flow, you find yourself actually enjoying the sensation of having a hint of energy. Combining exercise with a healthful diet and changes in your environment to bring greater stimulation and more rewards (positive reinforcement) can help you feel better and better, and you'll feel more and more inclined to exercise!

At the end of this chapter, one assignment suggests you start building a resource file of movements you'll enjoy doing to get moving. Here are a few ideas to get your thinking started:

- Dash up stairs to pull off all the sheets for the washer. Or hop on one foot if you have a single-level house.
- Race the clock to load the dishwasher. Be conscious of as much stretching as possible, bending over, reaching across the counter for the last glasses, playing white tornado as you wipe off the counter and table, jogging with high knees to the refrigerator with the food.
- Jog to the mailbox, or even sprint. If the box is attached to your house, run in place inside the front door, counting to 100, before you let yourself open the door.
- Do a dance you know (or don't know) to a song on the radio. The can-can is nice because it's a lot of exertion in a short time. An active disco or even a Charleston will get the juices moving. Be impulsive about this. Do it before you have time to talk yourself out of it. Have some fun!

Diet and Depression

The phrase "maintain a proper diet" ranks high on the most-boring-advice list. At the other extreme, health-food nuts find what they eat to be of consuming interest! Nevertheless, if your war against depression is to cover all fronts, you must be aware of the nutrients and chemicals you are putting into your body and what effects they may be having on your moods. High self-esteem includes getting to like your body and getting to like being nice to it by feeding it well for optimum performance. Cognitive therapy includes realizing the future consequences of what you put into your body each day. Be nice to your body and it will be nice to you; and you'll both be happier for it.

I'm always delighted when I hear of natural cures to health problems. Recent research on an amino acid called L-tryptophan suggests that this normal ingredient in a well-balanced diet could act as a natural anti-depressant. The brain uses it to manufacture serotonin, one of the necessary message-sending substances. Some people may be suffering depression from inadequate L-tryptophan in their diet. This substance can be found in brewer's yeast and in some supplementary vitamin formulas. If you are taking a vitamin complex, read the label to see if amino acids are included. Frequently, a "stress formula" or "total B-complex" tablet will contain it. And always check with your doctor before taking any medication, *especially* if you are already taking others. See Chapter 17 of David Burns' *Feeling Good* for an excellent "Consumer's Guide to Antidepressants."

The common stimulants, coffee, tea, and cola, are deeply imbedded in our cultural and everyday social rituals. Rather than consume them unthinkingly, you'll want to become aware of what they do to your body; it's just one more part of your anti-depression program. When you drink a cup of coffee, have a strong cup of tea, or down a cola, a measure of caffeine shoots through your bloodstream and the effect is stimulation to your system. The immediate effect usually seems satisfying. All these beverages do have an addictive effect, however, in the sense that it takes a greater and greater dose to get the same "up" result. If you're one who seldom drinks coffee, you've probably noticed that one cup on an empty stomach can leave you shaking all morning. You've known others who brag about drinking twenty cups every day. The important thing to know for depression is not that you can give yourself a shot in the arm this way, but that when the caffeine wears off, you'll feel more tired than ever. Hence the typical response is, "I need another cup" (to get back up). You'll probably find it more satisfying to seek your stimulation through more natural means (such as an intriguing project or some exercise) and save the occasional shot of caffeine for the times you really need it and have no other recourse.

If losing weight is one of your goals, you should know that caffeine stimulates the appetite for some people. Diets in most magazines allow you unlimited coffee and tea on the theory that there are no calories in these beverages. What they don't tell you is that if you happen to be one of those for whom coffee actually creates hunger, you're doing yourself in!

How does this work? Caffeine stimulates the adrenal cortex to produce its hormones, which in turn cause the liver to break down stored glycogen into glucose (a sugar), which flows into the bloodstream. You experience a lift from the higher blood sugar in your blood. Unfortunately, the insulin-triggering apparatus in the pancreas cannot distinguish between caffeine-stimulated sugar and food-digested sugar. The apparatus can become oversensitized and may overrespond to a normal stimulus. The resulting low blood sugar creates stronger hunger pangs. You may have noticed this effect if you've had coffee on an empty stomach and soon afterwards felt ravenously hungry. If you can avoid coffee, tea, chocolate, and colas, you can keep your system in better balance.

There are noncaffeine alternatives. Herb teas are now widely available in a variety of flavors. More and more soft drinks do not contain caffeine. Read the label. (A note for young mothers: If your children seem a little hyperactive, and they drink cola frequently, you might switch them to root beer, or better yet, natural fruit juices.)

Sugar is another product of our current culture receiving some attention and some criticism. The statistics on how many pounds of refined sugar each person in America consumes per year are staggering. You already know what sugar has to do with calories. But does sugar have anything to do with depression? Ultimately, eating a large amount of refined sugar tends to make you tired. You know how closely feeling tired is related to feeling depressed.

Here's how the sugar affects your body: When you eat, digestion converts food into glucose. All the carbohydrates convert into glucose, about half the protein does, and only 10% of the fat does. Normally the blood carries the glucose to the liver and it is then carried into the pancreas. There the increase in blood sugar stimulates insulin production. This insulin then goes to the liver, where it brings about the removal of excess glucose from the blood and begins to store it up as glycogen. During the time before the next meal the adrenal cortex hormones cause the liver to turn the glycogen into sugar, which circulates in the blood at the proper level. When your body gets a sudden dose of refined sugar, the insulin can overreact and cause too much sugar to be withheld from the blood. You may experience this reaction as a noticeable tiredness after the initial "shot" of energy. A tennis player who eats a candy bar for extra energy just before a game sometimes feels a dragging fatigue in the second set. If you have noticed this tendency, you may do better to eat several small, well-balanced meals throughout the day, avoiding caffeine, refined sugars, and processed starches like cake and pastries.

I describe the glucose-digestion process in detail not to recommend that you eliminate sugar from your diet entirely (unless such a project stimulates and motivates you as a cause worth pursuing), but to warn you against massive doses and the potentially depressing consequences. If you can substitute natural energy-giving foods, you'll have eliminated one more factor that may contribute to depression.

Carolyn explained to the group that she had discovered she could maintain a noticeably higher energy level by keeping her body well stocked with essential nutrients. She began to actually enjoy cultivating the habit of including fruits and vegetables, whole grains, and the meat and milk groups in her weekly plans. She found she was enjoying being good to herself in yet another way. Feeling fat is also depressing, and this program may help you lose weight, as a bonus. Several women in the housewives' group noticed that their "hunger" occurred in direct proportion to their boredom. When they were absorbed in a fascinating project, they even forgot to eat lunch. When nothing much happened all day to stimulate their interest, they "felt hungry" most of the day, even when they nibbled and ate regular meals. Creating stimulating activities may, therefore, not only help solve your depression, it may help you lose weight.

Getting enough fluids each day is an often-overlooked part of overcoming depression. The chemical balance in the nerve synapses seems to be maintained best when there is ample moisture in the body's system. Become aware of how much liquid you drink each day, and bring the level up to six to eight glasses of water a day as part of your overall program.

Readers with special problems such as diabetes should consult their physicians before significantly altering their diet, as should anyone who suspects a physical problem or who plans a major weight-loss or other special diet plan.

The Connection Between Body and Mind

Just as Thomas Edison was a long way from understanding microwave ovens and a blow-dryer in every home, we today are just on the frontier of understanding how our minds affect our body health and how body states affect our minds. The relationship between the body and depression is no doubt complex and I do not expect to provide all the answers. But looking more closely at some of the questions may provide some insight as you seek to understand how you can better take charge of overcoming your own particular form of depression.

Two examples of the interactions between body and mind have been mentioned above. One, illustrated by the rat experiment, was the possible chemical changes in the brain brought about by a more stimulating environment and the implications for lessening depression. The second example deserves more detailed discussion. It involves the lack of a stimulating environment or goal and low blood sugar. A boring task undertaken without emotional involvement is often more fatiguing than strenuous activity performed with interest and zest. As pointed out in the discussion above, a normal blood sugar level is maintained by a balance between insulin repressing the glucose level and the adrenal cortex hormones releasing glucose into the bloodstream. Enthusiasm and interest in your task stimulates the production of adrenal cortex hormones and keeps the blood sugar high enough for energy and alertness. When you simply "go through the motions" with a boring or routine task, this stimulation never occurs and the blood sugar level drops. The resulting fatigue makes you want to slow down even more, and the vicious circle continues. If you're depressed about feeling tired all the time, or feel tired because you're frequently depressed, it may be that a new interest in life—new projects, new goals—will have a biochemical effect for the better on your body.

Thinking Your Way to Health

Norman Cousins, retired editor of the *Saturday Review,* has raised some fascinating questions in recent years about the relationship between mind and body. He discusses several issues in other contexts that also seem to relate to the treatment of mild depression. Doctors who have corresponded with him emphasize that the physician must encourage the patient's own ability to mobilize the forces of body and mind to overcome the problem. The body does have a marvelous capacity to heal itself and then maintain health, if it receives proper nourishment and is relatively free from stress. This discussion reinforces the section above on proper diet. It also suggests that the depressed woman should monitor carefully her own expectations about what she and others "should" and "must" do. The body responds negatively to the high stress created by too many unfulfilled expectations.

Cousins' self-prescribed treatment included massive doses of both Vitamin C and laughter. The debate over the therapeutic value of Vitamin C rages on, but a factor that may have had a positive effect on his recovery from a crippling "irreversible" illness was his own *belief* in the effectiveness of Vitamin C. Many studies have shown that a patient's strong belief in a treatment can effect physical changes.

The great number of positive feelings generated by daily laughter may also have prompted healing. While a depressed person may have trouble seeing humor in even the silliest of scenes, women in mild depression may experience definite results from purposely exposing themselves to funny, whimsical, or delightful situations. Finding more to laugh at is a painless and highly recommended treatment. Fifteen minutes with Peg Bracken or Erma Bombeck could make your day. It'll certainly help you keep life in perspective!

The spiritual factor in healing is still not well understood. Whereas most people today would acknowledge that they believe in psychosomatic illness (your head or your heart bringing about physical illness), far fewer people would acknowledge the reverse process, often called faith healing (where your head or your heart helps bring about a physical cure). In reading the healing accounts of Jesus' ministry, we find the faith of the one healed to be a very important factor. Where people did not believe in his ability to cure, he could do very little. It would seem a patient's will to live and his or her belief in the possibility of recovery greatly affect the subsequent recovery.

How does this apply to depression? Much power is wrapped up in your own belief that you can and will overcome depression. If you insist on believing it is hopeless, you'll probably be right. If you believe instead in your own powers to take charge of your recovery, and believe changes are possible, you'll probably be right! Hope is a necessary spiritual element that seems to directly affect the biochemical responses of the body. Your ability to dream and to plan, to get excited about the future and to press forward, to take responsibility and to believe in yourself and an eternally loving God all combine to immeasurably affect the physical and chemical aspects of depression. You *can* change how you feel.

Suggested Assignments

1. Mood levels: Keep track in your journal of your mood levels, mapped against your menstrual cycle. Do this for

two to three months. Do your moods seem to be hormone-related? If so, what do you want to do about it? Exercise consistently, but particularly the last two weeks of your cycle? Get out of the house every day that last "low" week? If you have notable "up" cycles, how will you best take advantage of them?

2. Exercise: Start a resource file of movements that can get you started, such as those suggested on page 85.

- Enrolling in a fun exercise class can get you moving on days you'd otherwise succumb to the lazies. "Aerobic Dancing," created by Jacki Sorensen, now has classes in most major cities. The program is designed for non-dancers; you are taught fun and easy dance routines that are carefully planned to build up your heart and lungs (following Dr. Kenneth Cooper's Aerobics). More important for your motivation: Those who go have a lot of fun! Even Erma Bombeck reports klutzing her way through!

- Make a cassette tape. Choose your favorite lively songs, then add your own verbal instructions over the music, "Touch opposite toe, 1, 2, 1, 2; now run in place; step, kick . . ." Or buy an Aerobic Dancing record.

- Running is, of course, the least expensive sport, once you have some sturdy running shoes. The fact that there are now more than ten million women running says something about the appeal and the benefits. And more and more psychiatrists report improved results with patients who run.

- Check with your doctor if you have any suspected health problem. Start slowly so you won't get discouraged by unmet expectations. But by all means, get moving! Remember, the key word for counteracting sluggish nerve synapses is *stimulation*.

3. Diet: Observe your eating and drinking patterns over several weeks. Are you more dependent on coffee or sugar than you'd like to be? Are you drinking enough water? Would you like to lose some weight as part of your program? Draw up a reformed diet plan, being wary of setting unattainably high goals. Or design one new habit to work

on for twenty-one days. (Maxwell Maltz says it takes twenty-one days to establish a new habit.) Start small and build on your successes.

4. Mind and body: Record in your journal your responses to the section in this chapter on believing in your own healing. Choose a friend who seems to be positive most of the time. Ask her what keeps her going. See the book by Bruce Larson recommended below.

Suggested Readings

Bruce Larson, *There's a lot more to health than not being sick*. Waco, Texas: Word Books, 1981. An excellent, readable, and inspiring discussion of how to get our attitudes to positively affect our health and healing.

Norman Cousins, *Anatomy of an Illness as Perceived by the Patient: Reflections on Healing and Regeneration*. New York: W. W. Norton, 1979. Read this if you are interested in Norman Cousins' own story of recovery.

Jacki Sorensen, *Aerobic Dancing*. Totowa, N.J.: Rawson and Wade/Atheneum, 1979. A delightfully illustrated book to take you through Aerobic Dancing at home.

Mildred and Kenneth Cooper, *Aerobics for Women*. New York: Bantam Books, 1973.

David D. Burns, M.D., *Feeling Good: The New Mood Therapy*. New York: Signet, 1980. With a foreword by Aaron Beck, this is an excellent guide to Cognitive Therapy and would make a great companion book for a Breaking Through Group.

7

Your Mind

I first met Carolyn several years ago when a mutual friend brought her to our neighborhood Bible study class. At our next few meetings, I observed her as a woman of about thirty with prematurely silvered hair. Her clothes, hairdo, and makeup were always perfect, even if casual. She had enormous brown eyes and the kind of skin and cheekbones you see in makeup ads. She laughed easily, always seemed to have a smile for others, and made conversation effortlessly. All in all, she gave the impression of a very "together" person of many talents. It was only after a couple of months that Carolyn began to reveal how *she* saw herself: stumbling, floundering, out of control. Later on she described this period of her life as "a murky time. . . .I was full of insecurities. I didn't feel as if I counted."

Her actions at home reflected her uncertain attitude and her low self-image. She worried terribly about the impression she made, about the impression her home made, as if others' chance evaluations equalled her true value as a person. Occasional business entertaining for her husband sent her into anxiety attacks for a week ahead. Yet when we met in her home, it was exceptionally warm, graceful, and well-decorated, just as her personal appearance always was. We loved being with her and appreciated her contributions to the group.

Why the great discrepancy between the Carolyn we saw and the one she saw from the inside? Why could she not value the fine person we appreciated so much? Why did this negative image have so much control over her actions and feelings? How could such a smart person be so mistaken about reality? My amazement and puzzlement at these questions prompted a long study of the astounding power a person's self-image can have over her life.

The Problem: Self-Image and World-Image

Mental imaging's power over us is immense. The mechanism is so automatic, we usually aren't even aware of it. It sounds silly to *consciously* think to yourself, "I don't feel very confident today because my eyes looked a little baggy when I first got up, and I always get a yucky feeling when I have to rinse a diaper in the toilet, and I forgot to hem my dress, so I think I'll cancel on that luncheon I'm invited to today." Usually such decisions are made on the unconscious or only slightly conscious level. In mild depression, the awareness of low self-image is very vague. Most women I've interviewed don't think they have a low self-*image,* they just think they're less-than-adequate *people*! And, sadly, they usually act that way, which reinforces their mistaken belief.

How we perceive the "realities" outside ourselves also has an immense power over our subsequent behavior. These perceptions of the world can also greatly affect a state of depression. Jayne told of an experience that brought home the power of our *perception* of what is "really out there." She was staying with her friend Linda, who had signed up for an acting class in San Francisco. As Linda left, she said she was taking BART (Bay Area Rapid Transit) and would be home around 11:00 P.M. "Why aren't you taking your car?" Jayne asked. Linda responded, "Because I don't really know San Francisco well enough to find my way driving, plus it would cost too much to park." Jayne was astounded. For her, taking a car was highly preferable to public transportation in that situation. Linda was going to take a bus from the BART station, then walk several blocks to the class building, and return by the same path after dark. Jayne realized that her friend viewed driving along strange freeways and streets and paying a parking fee as far more intimidating than the bus transfer and night walk. Jayne said she would instead gladly study a map at length and negotiate any route in a car. Regardless of what the "true reality" was, each woman perceived a very different set of circumstances and consequently preferred entirely different paths of action. (A third woman might have decided not to take the class at all, because it was held at night clear across the bay.)

Much of the decision was based on how well each woman *imagined* she was able to cope with various aspects of the world she expected to enter. Jayne viewed herself as a skilled map reader. Linda saw herself as a brave and unintimidated nighttime walker, having just moved from an inner-city neighborhood. Jayne said she was a confessed coward when it came to strange neighborhoods at night. Linda prided herself on being thrifty by using public transportation. The "realities," if someone could measure them, are somehow irrelevant; what determines the situation is how each person perceives the realities. These perceptions form our feelings and influence subsequent behavior.

Another example of how our self-perceptions affect our opportunities and limitations is that a surprising number of adult women do not have their driver's licenses; a greater number do not venture far from home in their cars. Near the beginning of the housewives' classes, I astounded Carolyn by mentioning I would be delivering some papers to a city two hours away. She was admittedly frightened as she imagined herself driving that far alone. I thought her fears silly at the time because of my confidence in the trip. Two months later I had the same trembly feelings at the prospect of flying to New Orleans alone, finding my hotel, and going to a conference. Then I received a letter from an old college roommate telling of her three-week trip alone through Mali and Senegal in Africa. Clearly our perception of "the world out there" and our imagined ability or inability to handle it largely affects what we attempt and what we avoid.

When you're depressed, a cyclical erosion occurs. Your feelings of inadequacy make you perceive the world as more threatening than it is. The "threatening world" makes you perceive your skills for handling it as less adequate than they really are. You attempt less because you're intimidated by circumstances. Then you imagine (you think it's *true*) you are less capable because you haven't accomplished anything, haven't proved yourself, lately. Your self-confidence continues to erode and "the world out there" grows more intimidating.

The way to break this cycle is, first, to become aware of its potential power over you and, second, take decisive action.

Be aware of the areas of your life that you may have closed off. Do you catch yourself saying, "Oh, I just can't . . ."? Choose a particular action, step out into one of these scary areas, *do* the thing, and then consciously note the realities— perhaps in your journal. Most women find that they begin accumulating a list of "that wasn't so bad after all" responses. The limitations you feel today will evaporate tomorrow.

Paradigms

In a fascinating book called *Powers of Mind* Adam Smith helps us see a larger picture of how our perceptions work. He describes "paradigms" as the systems through which we interpret reality. What we are used to and have seen happen before is "true." When something comes along that is outside our paradigm, we feel uncomfortable. As a defense, since no one likes to feel uncomfortable, we may decide that a person or a possibility is weird, or immoral, or somehow bad. Or we ignore it as impossible.

Some of the backlash to the women's liberation movement can be interpreted as discomfort at the sight of a new paradigm. One woman I know said, "I could never ask Bill to skip his bowling night so I could go to a meeting." What about a hired sitter? "Oh, I couldn't do that; we only get sitters when we're both going somewhere together." Why? "That's just what we do." A paradigm. If this example seems tame or silly to you, how about flying to Atlanta to spend two weeks with old friends? Just you. The kids would stay home; your husband would pick them up at the neighbor's each night and cook dinner. Is this outside your frame of "reality"? So was rappelling down a cliff on Carolyn's Outward Bound trip. So was breathing without portable oxygen for Nancy. They thought it couldn't be done. But they did it. They constructed new paradigms for new realities.

We have to have paradigms in order to operate in our daily world without total confusion. We need to be able to assume that "chairs are sturdy" every time we sit down. The trick is to keep the right balance. Depression can result from taking too much for granted. But don't let your paradigms, your perception of reality, tie you down, make you feel cooped up, held back.

Self-Talk

How are your paradigms, or automatic mind-sets, maintained? How do you go about making the multitude of tiny decisions that make up your days? You do it by "self-talk." Your mind nearly always has some kind of "tape" running. "Let's see . . . where is the cleanser? Oh, here. (scrub, scrub) I wonder why Helen didn't come to our group yesterday?" Now your mind can choose one of two tracks: (1) "She's been sick a lot lately. Maybe I should call her and see how she's doing." Or (2) "Maybe she's mad at me and is trying to avoid me. Darn her. She's such a snob." The point for depression fighting is: Will you consciously *choose* the subjects of this self-talk? Or will you let it play on automatically?

Jayne became aware of her power over previously automatic tapes after she analyzed two typical mornings:

> When I'm beginning to get depressed some foggy, un-eventful-looking morning, I feel a little sluggish. So after the school bus leaves I slip back into bed with a book I want to finish. I get drowsy, so I let myself slip back to sleep. I wake up at ten o'clock feeling even more sluggish. I drag out of bed, strictly on guilt, not on ambition. As I contemplate dressing, I realize I'm feeling "fat." [She is 5'8" and weighs 135 pounds, so you can see how much of the problem is distorted self-image.] Suddenly I imagine I'm famished, and the thought of a large plate of french toast with hot cocoa flashes across my mind.

A second morning she took charge of each momentary decision:

> The alarm goes off at 6:45. I roll out of bed before I have a chance to start the "shall I or shall I not" debate. My immediate image of myself is of the sleek runner bounding through the silent neighborhoods while the air

still smells fresh. I slip into my nifty running shoes. Twenty minutes later I'm back, breathless, but tingly with energy. After a quick shower I slip into my nice jeans with the narrow waist, because I feel so trim . . . and noble! After the school bus leaves I sit down at my desk, with a glass of orange juice, to answer some letters, feeling sharp and alert. I don't notice any hunger until nearly noon. When I do have a late breakfast, my sinewy body wants only whole wheat toast, a hard-boiled egg, and milk.

What's the difference here? Same person. Same body. Same house. Same fog, not even noticed on the run. The difference is that at every step, every small decision point, the way Jayne pictured herself (alert athlete or hopeless slob) governed what she did next. And each image was self-perpetuating. The sluggishness bred inactivity. The movement bred more activity and energy. The difficult part of this situation is that when you're feeling low in energy, you don't *feel* like going running. You don't even feel like walking into the other room . . . unless it's to the refrigerator! It takes a certain inner resolution to break the old patterns and make the first movement to begin reprogramming the day's tape sequence. The self-management technique described in Chapter 4 can be useful for getting started, for taking the first steps to forming new patterns of thought and action.

Cognitive Therapy

An excellent method for reprogramming your self-talk, developed by psychologists such as Albert Ellis and Aaron Beck, is called *Cognitive Therapy*. It focuses on how we *think*, as opposed to how we act, or feel, or what our unconscious may have done to us. Cognitive Therapy has proven we *can* change how we feel and act by changing how we think. Ellis' basic theory for "Rational Emotive Therapy" is that what we think and what we believe *shapes* how we feel. One of Beck's great contributions is the discovery that depressed people frequently see life erroneously and thereby feel a great deal worse than they need to. Cognitive Therapy, then, is a way to correct your perceptions, thoughts, and beliefs about life and by doing so get rid of a lot of depression.

Beck divides the depressed person's misperceptions into three areas: a negative view of self, the outside world, and the future. The first includes self-blame, self-doubts, and the whole area of self-image, which will be discussed more fully in the next section. The second area includes a negative interpretation of the person's environment. It's very common, for example, to see the house and kids both actively working against you with tireless determination. A negative view of the future revolves around negative expectations, or hopelessness. Typically, you might hear, "It feels as if life is never going to get any better . . . as if it's always going to be this way."

Depressed people systematically distort their views of life in several ways. Beck has identified unconscious techniques he calls arbitrary inference, overgeneralization, magnification, and cognitive deficiency. It's easy, for example, to fall into making arbitrary inferences about who you are as a person. The self-talk would go something like this: "Sue hasn't called me in a week. She must really be mad at me. I must have done something awful to make her feel that way." The person has no objective information to lead her to this conclusion. When she catches herself in this discouraging thinking, she must learn to actively dispute such beliefs.

If she catches herself in an exaggeration or overgeneralization, such as, "I can *never* seem to get the laundry done. I'm really a lousy person to be so lazy and sloppy," she must learn some alternative statements. "I'm having trouble with the laundry right now, but that doesn't mean I can't change the situation. I think I'll try some problem-solving techniques and see what I can do about it."

Overgeneralizations about reality often occur when we unconsciously evaluate what we find around us. It can easily depress you to say, "Everyone I know is happy and well-adjusted and they're all so 'together' compared to me. They all keep their houses so nice." Disputing such misevaluation must include looking at the double standards you impose on yourself. You judge your friends' houses by the occasions when they know a group is coming over; you judge your own at its worst time when you wouldn't let anyone through the front door!

Making arbitrary inferences about the future, you might catch yourself saying, "I'll never be able to have any really close friends. No one wants the close kind of 'true through thick and thin' friendship that I'm looking for." To begin disputing, you can remind yourself you don't *know* what kind of friends people are really looking for, especially if you've never asked; you don't *know* who will move in down the block in three months; you don't *know* whom you'll get to know better a month from now. It's absurd to get depressed over hunches that you've made up in your head.

Magnifying the importance of a single event frequently deepens depression. Sue Ann fell into such a trap. She attended a party with her husband and some of his business associates. During the evening someone asked her a question. She misunderstood and answered in a way she later realized must have sounded rather strange. She felt foolish for months afterwards whenever she saw that person. The person probably would not even remember the party, much less the conversation if, as a reality check, you asked him a month later. As a way to dispute the possible overdramatization of a situation, ask yourself what *you* would think of another person in a similar situation. In this example, you'd probably scratch your head afterward and figure they must have misunderstood you. Then you'd dismiss it from your mind. At the very worst, you might think the person was a little spacy.

All these misconceptions can have a cyclical or spiral effect. Events stimulate erroneous thoughts, the thoughts create feelings, and the feelings affect future actions. For example, Lori may observe her "inability" to keep up with housework when her small son empties a kitchen drawer while she is putting the vacuum away. This conclusion provides a hopeless feeling, which Lori then generalizes to all housework for all time. She thinks to herself, "Why even try?!" She does no housework for the next two days, which further depresses her because her surroundings are so chaotic.

The way out of the cycle is to actively dispute such distorted thinking. Catch yourself in the self-talk; write it down and see how logical or reasonable it looks on paper. If it still seems reasonable, tell a friend what you're trying to do and ask her to help you analyze it to see if reality proves it out. If you're in a group, bring several self-talk statements to a meeting and let the group help you dispute them and find more reasonable and hopeful alternatives.

When you're helping someone else with a long-held belief, such as "I'll never get caught up on my housework," don't just argue with her by saying, "Sure you can. You can do it if you try." Instead, ask her to defend her belief: "How do you know you'll *never,* since no one can see into the future? Do you plan on never trying? How do you know you might not change your mind next week, when you get really sick of the mess?" Remind her (she may get annoyed with all your help!) that how she *thinks* about the problem will in large part determine what she *does* (or doesn't do) about it.

If you're working alone, write down a self-talk statement, then argue with it on paper. How do you know it's true? How can you prove Sue hates you just because she didn't call? How do you know it's not just because she has three kids home sick?

Check yourself. Do you systematically discount the good things that happen, ignoring the evidence that you, your world, and your future all hold some hopeful signs? At the same time, do you systematically keep track of and even magnify the negative evidence? You may want to start watching for and even writing down the positive bits and pieces of life, then training yourself to give less weight or importance to the negatives. If, for example, you do get the bathroom clean, or you have a particularly warm and satisfying conversation with a friend, you can send your thinking and self-talk in one of two directions: "There, I've done a good job in that room!" or "Darn! Still six rooms to go."

You have the power to choose how you'll feel by the way you evaluate yourself, your world, and your future. You *can* decide how deeply you'll let depression affect you or how you will take control over it more and more, as you work to combat it on yet another front.

We've looked at how self-image can be helped by not exaggerating events or circumstances in our mind, by choosing not to do a lot of self-blaming and self-deprecating. We turn now to some specific methods for improving your self-image.

Building Positive Self-Image

In order to significantly alter your self-image, you will need to focus on and become much more conscious of the good things about yourself and your situation. You must act, and then observe, and add the new information to your self-concept. ("Oh, yes, sometimes I *do* feel good after running!") At the end of this chapter you will be asked to list on 3x5 cards all the good things about yourself or your situation. You will then need to make time during your day to read over the cards. The idea here is first to direct your attention to the positive aspects, which you tend to overlook while depressed, and second, to focus on them regularly, not just when you are in the mood. For example, you could divide your "I'm good at it" cards into four stacks. One goes in the bathroom, one above the kitchen sink, one on the hall table, and one by the phone. Each time you use the bathroom, get a drink of water, pass through the hall, or finish a phone call, you stop and read the cards thoughtfully.

You will need to carefully avoid unfair comparisons that lead to pessimism. So often we compare the average parts of ourselves with the best in others. If you've just recently "discovered" ballet, it would be foolish to compare yourself with Margot Fonteyn. Yet you can be proud of yourself for ten minutes a day of ballet exercises done to the stereo. On your card, you can honestly say, "I'm getting to be a better dancer, and I am stretching and challenging my body every day."

If you're not convinced of the value of the assignment, you may be intrigued to learn about thankfulness. Of all the mental attitudes people can hold, the emotion of gratitude is most likely to generate healing in the body. Dr. Hans Selye's studies have found that gratitude is the mental state most likely to release the "healing juices" in the body. Thanking God for all you can think of can give you strength and ability you never knew you had. What a surprise that science has discovered what God knew all along!

Another specific action you can take to improve your self-image is to carefully monitor your actions. Lori has a maxim now: "I always try to go ahead and do whatever I would do if I were not depressed. Sometimes this means cleaning out a closet. Sometimes it's taking the baby for a walk." Another woman insists to herself that every morning she will get up and get dressed in something she wouldn't mind answering the door in, no matter who rang the bell. She puts on her going-out daytime makeup and does her hair. This particular woman also *enjoys* fifteen minutes of racing around picking up the living room. This practice adds to her self-image as an alert, organized, neat person. She feels better when these external, admittedly cosmetic touches have been attended to.

There is an important reason for carefully planning and carrying out intentionally positive and rewarding actions. If the only strokes (attention) you get are for that which you hold in low value (for example, housework), you're stuck. You must do that which you despise in order to get any reinforcement at all. You're like the ignored child who gets attention only when he is bad; so he decides getting punished is better than being ignored. Your only constructive alternative is to intentionally create situations that give you satisfaction and strokes. You must learn to be creative here for your own survival.

To counteract the strong tendency most women have to belittle themselves, I'm going to suggest something at the risk of creating another heresy in place of the old one. Draw your self-image on a graph. A horizontal line represents the ideal level of realistic self-esteem: not obnoxious or conceited, not shyly belittling. "Low self-image" is below the line and cocky is above it. If you're starting out now below the line, I'm suggesting you work up your self-confidence until you're somewhere *above* the line. Be daring and err in the other direction for a while. Become a little cocky! Once you have a solid feel for what it means to know you are a worthwhile person, to know you are good at things, valuable regardless of what you do, then you'll be able to temper it a little and level off. Don't worry about arrogance. Circumstances will come along to knock you down soon enough. Better that you be up there somewhere when that happens than already down.

You'll probably feel uneasy for awhile with this new norm of so much self-confidence that you feel cocky. But learning to recognize and acknowledge your strengths is an essential part of overcoming depression.

Carolyn's journal one year after the housewives' course exemplifies a self-confidence worth striving for.

> I am in a state of loving myself! I find it enables me to reach out to others, to offer myself, whereas earlier I felt myself to be less than adequate and that reaching out was presumptuous.

In a later entry she notes,

> Meeting risks is a positive challenge to me now rather than a fearful proposition. I am making efforts to try new things, and I now realize that the fear of failure is only my fear of someone else's disapproval.

This is the kind of attitude that can make life exciting . . . and meaningful. And it quickly crowds out depression.

In your small group you can do wonders to raise each other's self-images. You will want to train yourselves to express compliments and strokes out loud. So often we notice a friend looking especially good, but we don't say it. In an anti-depression support group, the by-word is *say it*. And when you are on the receiving end, *believe it*. You will need to form a pact. For example, if a woman, in response to a compliment about her outfit, says "Oh, this old thing," everyone must immediately call her to account. "Dorothy, *you look great!*" Stop her and make her say, "Thank you." Keep each other honest. One reason we have trouble accepting compliments (and gifts) is that we don't really believe we're worth it. Believe it! You're worth it!!

One final note: You are not a bad person if you can't get out of depression. Do not be caught in the trap of believing you are okay only when you're "on top of it." You need not stay away from your group if you're down and have no "success story." What better time to come than when you need help?

Images of Anger

Before we move into the final section on psychological self-awareness, we should consider one negative and often hidden cause of depression: anger. Buried anger is one of the most elusive factors in housewives' depression because we, as women, are trained to bury it so well. Women are raised to be "nice." Christian women are expected to be *very* nice . . . and slow to anger besides. Yet many theorists on clinical depression suggest that unexpressed anger can be a cause of depression.

If you were to ask a roomful of mildly depressed housewives, "Do you feel anger about something?" a few might acknowledge, "You're darn right I'm angry!" And they'd go on to detail their grievances. But a greater number of the women would say no, they feel no anger. When pressed, they would probably begin to describe feelings more along the lines of numbness, listlessness, apathy. These "non-feelings" seem to be the farthest thing from the adrenalin-producing feelings of anger and rage. If you pressed even further, however, you might begin to uncover some masked feelings of resentment or discouragement toward their circumstances. Often such feelings are hard to pin down, even harder to admit, because the counterfeeling wells up, "I shouldn't feel this way; I have no right to complain."

Jayne was a typical example of buried anger. She was not even aware of it herself for some time. She had heard the theory: Depression is sometimes anger turned inward because the person thinks the outward expression is unacceptable. But she didn't "feel" that this theory could be true at all in her own case. After many months she began to acknowledge her resentment of her nice home in the suburbs, her two lovely children, her kind and hardworking husband. She resented *having* to be there. She resented the choice she'd made to marry right after college and give up her freedom to live her own life. Simultaneously she felt guilty for having such feelings. After all, she reminded herself, "few people in this world have it this well. I *ought to* be appreciating this. I ought to be grateful I don't have to work, that my children are healthy, that my husband doesn't drink or beat me." Her feelings of resentment *were real,* nevertheless. The "oughts" didn't help. When she finally allowed herself to acknowledge these feelings, she was able to deal with them openly and she came noticeably closer to controlling her depression, instead of letting it control her.

When Jayne realized how real her regrets were for not having lived another, "more stimulating" life, she began to look around for alternatives. She was, in effect, saying, "Given the fact that I am where I am now, what am I going to do about it?" She realized she really did love her husband, her children, her home, her great freedom to set her own schedule, the liberty in not having to report to work somewhere each day. She began to create some freedoms within the setting she chose to remain in. Over the next couple of years, she found channels for the talents she was discovering. She took occasional trips out of town in what turned out to be a part-time consulting job. As a practical matter, those few days away from the family now and then provided an outlet for the immense energy she discovered she'd had all along—energy she'd been stuffing down into the "I'm not angry" bag before.

Jayne exemplifies a cycle we all fall into when anger is a factor in our depression. Jim Petersen, a Portland minister, has described a cyclical pattern. The cycle begins with a particular expectation. Jayne expected life to be challenging, rewarding, and satisfying. She became aware of a sense of loss when she thought about her housekeeping duties and how they seemed to keep her from a more stimulating life. Her primary feeling was one of frustration and irritation, mixed with disappointment. These feelings then "flopped over" into anger, the secondary response to the loss. But she was "a good Christian" and a nice woman, and she knew she shouldn't be angry, so she immediately suppressed it. Keeping the anger suppressed produced fatigue and guilt. And the depression increased. She was then off on another expectation and the cycle repeated.

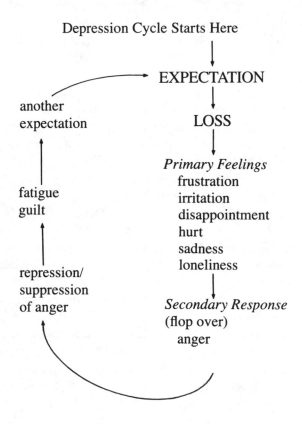

Depression Cycle Starts Here

EXPECTATION

LOSS

another
expectation

Primary Feelings
frustration
irritation
disappointment
hurt
sadness
loneliness

fatigue
guilt

repression/
suppression
of anger

Secondary Response
(flop over)
anger

Another common example: Carolyn expects her son home at 2:45 from the bus stop. Her expectation is not being met and she experiences a sense of loss. At three o'clock she begins to fear for his safety. She is worried, fearful, sad, perhaps disappointed at not seeing him coming up the driveway. He finally appears at 3:10 with a handful of flowers. The "flop over" is immediate—she flies into a rage. "Where have you been?!!" When he explains he was just picking her some flowers along the way, she suppresses her anger and tries to be understanding. Later she is aware of feeling fatigue, guilt, and an overall sense of depression. Such phrases come to mind as, "Why do I get angry at him so easily? He's only eight." She does not associate her general feeling of "being a bad mother" with her listless feeling the rest of the afternoon. Nevertheless, she is busy setting up another expectation that may or may not be met: that her husband will arrive home precisely at six for her carefully prepared meal. The cycle begins again when the freeway is jammed and the dinner gets cold.

How can the cycle be broken? The best way is to become carefully aware of the expectations you build. *Expecting* things of other people is a controlling approach. *Hope* is less demanding. Expectations are often rigid. Hope can be more flexible and understanding. "I'd like to serve dinner at six, but I won't *expect* to." Righteous indignation is a "master" approach. The biblical "servant" approach takes a frank look at what is real (and realistic) and tries to love the world into something better.

If you slip and find yourself at the disappointed stage, express the hurt. Let out the primary feeling. "Yes, I really did look forward to a quiet dinner while the sun was just going down . . . I missed you." Or, "I was really scared that something had happened to you on the road." Or, as Jayne might have expressed, "I'm sad and disappointed at the life I have missed as a bright, young career person." We are counseled by the scriptures to be slow to anger. Nevertheless, if you slip to this next step and you *are* angry, acknowledge it. "By golly, I *am* angry!!" Beware of unconsciously burying it with half-believed "shoulds."

If you find yourself depressed for no apparent reason, check back through the steps in the cycle. "Where was I before I was angry? Oh, I was disappointed at having missed. . . ." Or, "I felt hurt that. . . ." Identify and express your way back through the cycle until you come to your original expectation. Decide whether it was fair and reasonable. Go through the steps backwards in your mind and deal with the realities of the situation along the way. "Yes, he did want to surprise me with that handful of flowers." Or, "Freeway traffic is something no person can count on."

Your moods can have great effect on your expectations, and therefore upon your depression. When you are tired and irritable, do you expect people to clear a path for you? Are you more tolerant and patient when you're at a higher energy level? Do you hold less demanding expectations of others and yourself when you're feeling good about yourself? Do you express impatience with others when you're most impatient with your own perceived failures? When you're angry at yourself for being childish, do you expect the children to act more like adults? Keeping a log in your journal will help you become more conscious of your responses.

To summarize, anger is the result of unfulfilled expectations. Anger comes in direct proportion to the gap between your expectation and the reality as it turns out. The amount of anger buried will be roughly equivalent to the depression you experience.

Images of Growth

From time to time, I try to get an avocado seed to root. The last one that sprouted sent out a healthy supply of roots into its waiting container of water. But the new plant grew too fast for the jar I had chosen. Before I knew it the white roots were tangled in jumbled circles in the bottom of the jar. I had trouble easing them out when I finally transplanted the seed into potting soil. Plants contain a force—they *must* grow. They will grow in spite of all efforts to contain them. Tree roots crack sidewalks. Thistles overtake pastures. Sunflowers grow so fast you can watch them change daily. Avocado roots grow around in circles if they must, but they keep growing.

We are more like plants than we usually acknowledge. We hold the mistaken idea that people stop growing when they reach their full physical height. We overlook the far more miraculous and exciting lifelong growth of the spirit and the mind. Nothing delights us more than to hear of a seventy-year-old woman who has just graduated from college . . . or run a marathon. Yet we continually downplay our own needs to seek new experiences, to challenge ourselves, to seek a "larger pot in which to grow." Somehow we continue to imagine things should stay pretty much the same from here on. One of the deformities women experience from "too small a jar" is depression.

The woman who wants to move beyond the confining world of depression will need to actively seek new ways to grow and to reach out toward her full potential. If lack of stimulation contributes to her depression, she will need to seek constructive forms of stimulation. If a feeling of powerlessness contributes to her feelings of hopelessness, she will need to actively take charge of her own growth process until she feels she does have some control over her destiny. If a lack of physical movement is part of her problem, she will want to seek challenging action activities in order to develop a lifelong interest in exercise.

The need to grow has been classified in many ways. Among the most popular classifications is the "hierarchy of needs" developed by Abraham Maslow. His theory has been arranged into a pyramid of the various needs that motivate us all.

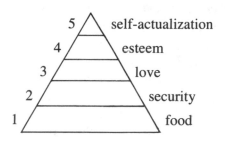

Maslow observed that in our most basic state we are motivated by the need for food and shelter. When it is satisfied, our attention turns to safety and security (Level 2). When we feel fairly secure, we notice that we have a need for love from others and a desire to belong, to feel accepted by others (Level 3). When these needs are largely met, we look to self-esteem and esteem from others (Level 4). We may seek status or recognition, praise, or the rewards of holding office. Self-actualization (Level 5) is the highest level in Maslow's scheme.

The theory suggests that as long as a lower need is largely unsatisfied, you will not be particularly aware of the higher needs. That is, if your house burns down, you'll forget your interest in art until adequate shelter is arranged. It's also important to realize there is no "ought" structure to this analysis. You shouldn't feel guilty for operating near the bottom of the pyramid. You simply *are* where you are at this time.

Maslow suggests that challenge (stimulation) is a necessary precondition in our environment in order to live and move up this pyramid. We have noted already the disastrous depressing effects a lack of stimulation can bring. It is also interesting to visualize the needs pyramid as a "mountain" to be climbed. Women were once taught to be content with shelter, safety, and love needs. Now women are seeking the challenges of growth into esteem and self-actualization.

Unlike the resignation Freudian psychology often induces ("It was all formed in your infancy; it's all in your subconscious") or the despair the strict behaviorist psychologists can instill ("We're all programmed by our environment; all our choices are preconditioned"), Maslow's approach, and the school of psychology that is based on that approach, emphasizes the positive growth that can happen to an individual. This is a psychology of hope. Growth is as much a basic need as salt or Vitamin C. If housewifery suppresses growth, it may indeed be as destructive as a Vitamin C deficiency. As a person moves up the pyramid, she experiences, according to Maslow, certain growth needs: aliveness, beauty, completion, effortlessness, goodness, justice, perfection, playfulness, richness, self-sufficiency, simplicity, truth, uniqueness, wholeness. By focusing on these needs, and the positive outlook that working on them can bring, women can discover additional tools for moving from depression to new growth.

Let's assume for a moment that your basic needs for food and safety are satisfied. Your feelings of being loved and accepted may be all right, or they may be a little thin (it's pretty easy to feel taken for granted as a homemaker). And we'll assume you're planning to put the earlier part of this chapter to work to increase your self-esteem. How, then, can the housewife begin to create opportunities to satisfy the growth needs?

The following pages offer a potpourri of ideas for you to grow on. Just as at a buffet, don't feel you must choose every one. Be selective; decide what is most helpful to you.

Aliveness is, in a way, what we have been talking about throughout this book. Our whole program is designed to eradicate deadness, increase self-regulation, encourage spontaneity. When you have reached a certain threshold of recovery, your senses will begin to attune to little serendipities. You might notice the smell of the early morning air, study the colors of a passing butterfly, examine the crystal patterns in window ice, or see the sculptured qualities of a bare tree against a lead sky.

Beauty comes very close to aliveness. It's also very close to thankfulness. As your list in your "thanks" card file grows, you'll feel more sharply the beauty in what is around you, previously taken for granted: children who giggle when they wrestle (you'll feel less tense about the nearby lamp); the faint popping sound of a spider web breaking against you as you pass by the hedge.

Completeness is one of the most difficult for a housewife to experience. By the very nature of her job, nothing is ever "done." Rugs always seem to need vacuuming, sinks never stay clean. It takes a particular inventiveness to create opportunities to finish something. Some women find great delight in needlepoint, or pottery, or even canning, because they know when they've finished. Raising children isn't that way. If you sense a need for some completeness in your life, design some small situation in which you can be satisfied by a small accomplishment.

Effortlessness may be sought but, again, it is an elusive goal in the average home. It comes to the fore when your talents begin to mesh well with the tasks you've chosen. One woman discovered dance after her three children were born. In her ballet exercises she felt at home for the first time with an activity that truly suited her instincts. While the dancing was hard work, it was effortless in the sense that she felt very much at peace while she did it. More often we enjoy effortlessness watching others exercising their gifts: a gymnast leaping above the balance beam, a horse and rider taking a jump, a typist turning out a perfect page. We can seek out and appreciate these experiences, once we identify the need we feel to experience them.

Goodness and *justice* arise when we witness someone being victimized, and we have energy for the first time in years to come to their aid. Some women have become adamant consumer advocates. Others volunteer at a juvenile detention center. Some sponsor a child abroad; others tutor reading.

Perfection has a dark side, as well as an energizing one, for housewives. We all know at least one woman who gets depressed because her house is never perfect, even though you or I might judge it quite suitable for the average tea honoring Queen Elizabeth. If too-high expectations for yourself are at the heart of your depression, be wary of allowing perfection to be high on your list of growth needs. You may want to emphasize spontaneity instead for a while. Perfection can, however, be a delightful source of new energy for some women. If you've never quite managed to get the whole house clean in one day, because someone is always messing up the territory you've just completed, you might consider drastic measures like a whirlwind cleaning lady to come in for one day while you take the children to the zoo. Or send the kids to a friend's house and work alongside the paid housefairy. Such surprise doses of perfection, even when short-lived, can do wonders for morale for weeks afterward.

Playfulness . . . humor . . . sheer joy at the silly and the surprises in life—all these are difficult to plan for, but you can create fertile situations in which they'll be more likely to happen. How often do you go to the beach, the river, or the park? When was the last time you built a sand castle? (I don't mean helping your child, I mean one of your very own.) Or rolled down a grassy slope? Or held hands as you walked with your husband? Or hummed out loud at the grocery store?

Richness means noting the fresh smell of the air in the early morning, after a first rain, or in the fall evening when wood burning in fireplaces reminds you of camping. Richness means being stimulated by the simple genius of an Aaron Copland symphony. Richness is one scoop of French vanilla ice cream, licked very slowly.

Self-sufficiency evokes twinges of guilt or distaste in some women. "I'm supposed to depend on my husband" or, "I'm supposed to depend on the Lord," they insist. The need for self-sufficiency here means that if you were suddenly widowed, you could cope with the contingencies. Autonomy, a related need, means that people call *you* to serve on committees, not just to see if you'd ask your busy husband if he can serve. Self-determination means asking your husband's opinion out of love and consideration for him, rather than getting his approval. Self-sufficiency doesn't deny the other person in your marriage, it gives him a richer, fuller person to be married to. Self-sufficiency doesn't deny God, it gives him an infinitely more capable servant to do the work set out for you.

Simplicity is the bare essence. Emily Dickinson's poems. Hemingway's economy of words. It's honesty. Capturing your true feelings in a single gesture or one word. When you see simplicity, you know it. It can be Picasso's handful of flowers, framed on a bare white wall, the slightly mangled daisy your son brings you, a kiss so light it makes the hair stand up on the back of your neck.

Truth is pure and clean, straightforward and honest. It's leveling with yourself about how you really feel. It's telling your journal, even if you don't dare tell anyone else. It's getting to the essence of a concern with a friend, when before you've always done a polite minuet with her. Truth has no substitutes.

Uniqueness is something you'll begin to relish as your self-image grows. You will begin to appreciate the ways you're *unlike* any other person in the world. As you begin to feel more accepted and worthwhile wherever you go, you'll feel less tense about the imagined need to conform to everyone else and their expectations. And you'll begin to enjoy more and more the idiosyncrasies in others you meet. Your friends may become more varied after a while, in turn producing more stimulation for you, more growth, more aliveness.

Wholeness is seeking integration of all the parts of yourself. It's being connected to your feelings and your actions. It's experiencing inner peace when that connectedness starts to happen. It's living with the ambiguities and paradoxes of life so that they bring interest and fascination rather than discomfort and unrest.

You've just read a hint of what self-actualization is about. The descriptions are not intended to be exhaustive, just suggestive to spark your imagination. In order to grow and to maintain mental and physical health as a human being, you will want to be trying to fulfill some of these needs. You already know the consequences of neglecting them.

The human potential movement has made important and much-needed contributions in recent years. But for all its truth and beauty, self-actualization is not the last word. People, particularly women who are depressed, will want to look beyond individual growth. There is more to life than feeling good. Self-actualization is a step toward broader goals. It is the middle of the book, not the final chapter.

Suggested Assignments

1. Cognitive Therapy. There are many ways to get in touch with self-talk—a necessary step in getting rid of depressing feelings originating in our heads. One method is to keep paper and pencil near the main areas where you work and jot down verbatim some of the thoughts you find running through your mind. See if you can "catch" yourself in thoughts you didn't realize you were thinking. See if patterns emerge over a week or two.

   Another method involves writing down your "never" and "always" statements. Example: "Bobby *always* leaves his boots on the laundry room floor." "No one *ever* calls me to go anywhere." Take time to actively dispute these statements on paper; if you don't believe yourself in your disputing, do it with a friend who can see other possibilities.

   Thirdly, read again the section on Cognitive Therapy, then look systematically through your own self-talk for examples of making arbitrary inferences, overgeneralizations, etc. Doing this with a friend, or in pairs in your group, is more effective than working alone.

2. Getting started on self-image. You will need a whole package of 3x5 cards. Divide them into three stacks. With the first stack begin a list: *Things I Do Well.* List one to a card. See if you can list five the first day. Add five more in the following week. Set a reward for the one who brings the longest list to the group. The second list: *Things I Like About Myself.* Include character traits and other intangibles different from the things you do well. The third list: *Things I'm Thankful For.* Include things beyond yourself as well as personal things, e.g., good health, safe neighborhood, hardworking husband, nation at peace, the daily newspaper, a well-stocked supermarket, a good friend _____ (name), freedom. (Note: Clinically depressed patients tend to *rate* their own performance lower, even when they perform as well as or better than non-depressed patients. They are also much more pessimistic about the likelihood of succeeding, evidence to the contrary. Beware of slipping into this. Take advantage of good friends who can help keep you honest!)

3. Affirmations can consciously reprogram your self-talk tapes. Begin by noting on paper a few areas you feel good about and/or want to grow in. Then write out affirming statements on your blank cards. Examples: "I have a hopeful attitude toward the future and I know I will accomplish my goals." "I develop feelings of self-respect and esteem in others." "I easily and generously show warmth and concern to the people I meet." "I am honest with myself; I am honest with others." Remember, this exercise should not deepen your discouragement or produce a feeling of hypocrisy. Affirmations are meant to put you on a different path than the one you've been on. If the above list seems a bit much, choose one negative self-talk statement you'd like to get rid of, rephrase it in the positive, and start saying it to yourself. You *can* make this tool work for you if you decide to.

4. A positive self-image relies, more than we like to admit, on the feedback we get from others. Believing that we're loved and accepted as-is is difficult until we are affirmed by others. For the isolated housewife, this means getting

with others so the feedback can happen. Action is the only way to make it happen. Choose some new activity, however insignificant, and go *do it.*

As a corollary, look for sincere ways of affirming others, particularly those in your group. "I really appreciate your _____."

5. Write out a list of the expectations you have of yourself, your family, or your immediate environment, that you feel are going unmet. Using your journal, explore what you feel when you go down this list: disappointment? genuine grief at something missing? irritation? frustration? hurt? loneliness? Respond on paper to your feelings, "Yes, I feel really hurt when _____." Does your tone turn to anger? If you get in touch with stronger feelings underneath, write this out too, "Yes, darn it! It really sends me up the wall when _____!" At this point a good friend who is willing to embark on the same assignment may be crucial. Tell each other (or your group) what you've discovered.

Once you have unearthed and expressed this buried anger, you are free to go back and look analytically at your expectations. As a practical matter, you may decide to disengage yourself from "justice" for a while. Temporarily backing off may free you for a fresh approach.

6. Using a purse-size spiral notebook, or a stack of 3x5 cards, write down the growth needs listed in this chapter, one to a page (aliveness, beauty, etc.). Once each day, preferably in the morning, read over the list. Then try to be aware of how one of these features can be present in your life. As you discover one, write the experience down briefly in your notebook on that page. Keep the notebook going for several months, until you're noticeably more aware of these aspects of your life.

One final note: Self-awareness is a lifelong project. Even the exercises suggested here involve far more than one week's work. Settle on your own pace—that which best serves your own spirit—ambitious enough to keep you moving, slow enough to allow for genuine change.

Suggested Readings

David D. Burns, M.D., *Feeling Good: The New Mood Therapy*. New York: Signet, 1980.

Albert Ellis, *A New Guide to Rational Living*. North Hollywood, Calif.: Wilshire Book Co., 1975. The classic text on Rational Emotive Therapy. A clear guide for thinking your way out of negative self-talk.

Maxwell Maltz, *Psycho-Cybernetics*. North Hollywood, Calif.: Wilshire Book Co., 1978. A classic on the subject of getting control of your life, with a comprehensive system for remaking your self-image.

John Powell, S.J., *Fully Human, Fully Alive*. Niles, Ill.: Argus Communications, 1976. A delightfully readable little handbook on cognitive therapy.

Robert Schuller, *Discover Your Possibilities*. New York: Ballantine Books, 1978. The prophet of possibility thinking. I consider his contribution one vital step in overcoming depression.

Betty Friedan, *The Feminine Mystique*. Chapter 13.

PART THREE

Looking Ahead
to Permanent Change

8

Discovering Your Gifts and Talents

The housewives' class had been meeting for a couple of months
when Gwen began to speak of her restlessness. "I still feel
stuck, somehow. I feel like I need to start seeking wider horizons. I've learned to live day by day, even week by week.
Now I can cope, and I'm ready for more. What hopes and
dreams are out there? What more is out there for my life?"

As the discussion evolved, the women realized that they
were not only ready but eager to develop some more meaningful activities in their lives. The group was really asking
life-planning questions. The issues were "Where do we go
from here?" and "How do we get there?"

I suggested to the group that activity for its own sake was
fine as a temporary measure to get beyond the inactivity of
depression, but a more permanent answer lay in the uniqueness
of each individual. "Each one of you," I explained, "has a
special collection of abilities and interests, perhaps still un-
developed, which I'll call your gifts and talents. Only when
you discover these and begin to develop them will you begin
moving beyond day-to-day coping." I suggested that each woman
in the room would need to begin planning a portion of her life
around the gifts she would be discovering.

This chapter presents a basic outline for your own adventure
into discovering your own best self.

Getting Perspective

In order to give yourself the proper perspective for your future
and to pinpoint where "now" really is, you'll want to draw
a lifeline graph, just as the women in the first class did. Draw
an eight-inch horizontal line, marking off an inch for every

ten years. Label every tenth year since your birth. Indicate above the line major milestones in your life, such as your own youth, student days, wedding, career, motherhood, and stages beyond. Then on separate parallel lines below your lifeline, add significant points along the way for your husband(s) and children.

As you develop your own lifeline graph, you'll become aware of the various stages women often go through. Because housewives' depression can occur during any of these stages, it's helpful to be aware of the main characteristics of each. A stage itself may not be the primary cause of depression, but your being aware of the possible contributing effects can help you ward off added problems. Only the most common stages are discussed here; an assignment at the end of the chapter will help you write your own personal version of this section.

Stages of Life

Young Mothers

Women who find themselves at home with small babies are frequently surprised by depression. They may not even realize that the dull, listless, sometimes hopeless feelings they experience actually constitute mild depression. If they have come from a stimulating environment such as a career or college life, no one has warned them that baby-tending is an isolated existence. No one thought to mention that they'd have to think up and plan all contacts with other adults. No one told them just how many diapers there would be, how unceasingly tiny people eat, how toys have lives of their own and make their way out onto the floor whenever backs are turned.

When Lori drew her life out on a graph, she was astounded. She had been convinced, unconsciously, that baby-tending was going to last forever. She'd never actually stopped to think that she would someday be the mother of teenagers, that they would then be gone and she would be just forty-four years old. After hearing Sue Ann's story of being surprised by a nearly empty nest, Lori was thankful that she'd been alerted about what lay ahead. She resolved to begin right then to build for the second life she would be starting midway through her lifetime. As she probed her own interests, she discovered education could be for her a lifelong pursuit, not a one-time, four-year experience. She realized that continued learning would provide one needed source of stimulation amidst the babies.

Mothers of School-age Children

The week the last child goes off to first grade marks the beginning of a stage of mild depression for many women. For the first time in six or ten years, the house is empty and quiet from eight to three each day. Some women fail to grasp the impact such a change is going to have on their lives. They're bewildered at suddenly having time on their hands. Everyday household tasks that used to take all day because of constant interruptions now can be done by 10:30. And then what for the rest of the day? Other women anxiously await their "day of liberation" with an armful of plans for activities they'll finally have time for. But the depression hits later when they begin to realize an endless round of tennis and redecorating is hardly more satisfying, ultimately, than was the laundry folding.

Mothers with Empty Nests

Much has been written about the rude awakening women are having these days when their children leave home and the women suddenly have the second half of life facing them, with nothing particular to do. The impact cannot be understated. Longer life spans, low maternal death rates at childbirth, and fewer children to raise all mean that millions of women today face some forty years without children at home. The whole question of a loss of identity is raised when women are no longer needed by the most significant people in their lives.

A woman named Rose told of the day she drove her last daughter off to college. "Becky and I made the seven-hour drive alone. On the way home it really hit me out of the blue. 'She's at school now. I'm not Mother anymore. Who *am* I?'

For several months after that I couldn't 'hear' my husband saying I was still wife, if not mother. I guess because you feel a loss, you don't think about all the rest you still have. It's true, of course, you do go on being mother, but it's never the same. Whenever they come back home, they come as guests. They're no longer dependent on you and on what you have to give them. Your special role has evaporated."

Rose went back to school, to become a professional counselor, but not before several years of struggle, trying to discover what her unique gifts and talents were.

The Migrating Wife

When "the company" transfers a man and his family every few years, the wife sometimes experiences a depression of rootlessness. Or depression caused by some other force, such as chemical changes, may be accentuated by the continual moving. No matter what chronological life stage a woman happens to be in, having to leave friends and relationships behind and begin anew, over and over, makes the task of overcoming depression that much more difficult and challenging. A woman may feel even more hesitant in a new town to take the initiative of seeking out a support group. Close and trusting friends are rarely found quickly. It takes more initiative and more determination for the corporate-transfer wife to survive. The feelings of being "at the company's bidding" can add to the feeling of powerlessness. The antidote is to take charge of as much of life as possible. Plan activities, and then *do* them. Plan that last year of work toward a degree, and then enroll. Plan ways to make friends quickly, and then get out of the house and do them. The other principles in this chapter apply to the migrant wife, but the frequent moving means you'll have to jump in sooner and live with more determination, or nothing will ever happen!

There are innumerable variations on the corporate-transfer-wife theme. The abrupt life-changes stage can happen at any age. The pastor's wife whose husband goes into counseling or teaching finds she no longer has an accompanying role, with its built-in expectations, duties, friends, and automatic status.

The political wife whose husband loses an election or returns to business is abruptly left without the myriad campaign and social activities that gave her identity, excitement, and purpose. The woman who has lost a job she held for years suddenly finds herself at home much more than she likes. In all these cases, depression brought about by a noticeable loss of role or purpose means the woman must take charge with that much more determination if she is to survive to live a meaningful life of her own.

No matter what state you are in now, your lifeline graph reminds you that you are in process, in a state of change, moving away from some parts of life and always into new experiences. Newness, discovery, and growth produce the positive energy that can dispel depression. As you learn about your potential gifts and talents, keep in mind the stages of life ahead of you. They can provide a framework within which you can visualize and plan your own development and movement.

Career Research

"I really don't know where to begin."

"I just don't *feel* talented at anything."

"You don't know what a klutz I am at whatever I try." Common responses from housewives. Others say, "Okay, I'm competent in math, but what possible good does that do me while I have two toddlers to care for?"

John Holland, the career guidance expert, whose work has been made even more popular by Richard Bolles' *What Color Is Your Parachute?* has provided an excellent method for looking at yourself and your abilities. Although there are any number of ways to go about discovering your talents, Holland's system is explained here in some detail to provide a specific, tangible starting point. The scheme provides resources for you to accumulate evidence of your own unique cluster of interests and potential abilities.

Along with the many who have followed his lead in the career guidance field, Holland has divided personalities into six categories. The six personality types are: Realistic, Conventional, Enterprising, Social, Artistic, and Investigative.

The following hexagon illustration indicates some of the characteristics for each personality type. You may find yourself easily in one category. More likely, you'll find some of yourself in each section. Try to see which two or three categories include the greatest number of words that describe you. Which section seems *most* nearly you? Which one or two sections seem most unlike you?

As with all theoretical models, this chart simplifies the human personality. The point is to give you new insights into forms and possibilities, not to lock you into a category. If it helps you see yourself a little more clearly, then it's useful to play "the hexagon game."

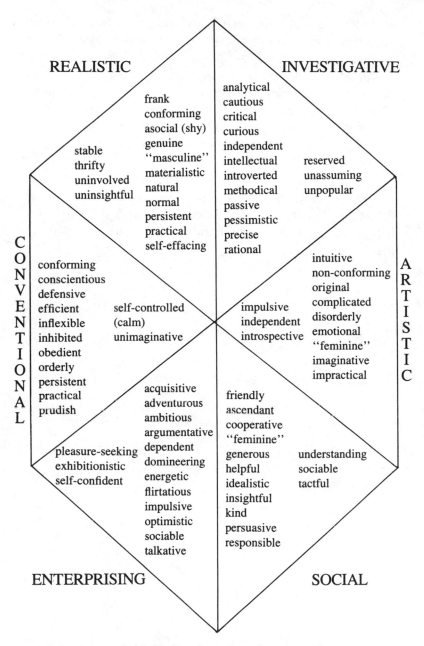

REALISTIC   INVESTIGATIVE

frank
conforming
asocial (shy)
genuine
"masculine"
materialistic
natural
normal
persistent
practical
self-effacing

analytical
cautious
critical
curious
independent
intellectual
introverted
methodical
passive
pessimistic
precise
rational

stable
thrifty
uninvolved
uninsightful

reserved
unassuming
unpopular

CONVENTIONAL

ARTISTIC

conforming
conscientious
defensive
efficient
inflexible
inhibited
obedient
orderly
persistent
practical
prudish

self-controlled
(calm)
unimaginative

impulsive
independent
introspective

intuitive
non-conforming
original
complicated
disorderly
emotional
"feminine"
imaginative
impractical

acquisitive
adventurous
ambitious
argumentative
dependent
domineering
energetic
flirtatious
impulsive
optimistic
sociable
talkative

friendly
ascendant
cooperative
"feminine"
generous
helpful
idealistic
insightful
kind
persuasive
responsible

pleasure-seeking
exhibitionistic
self-confident

understanding
sociable
tactful

ENTERPRISING   SOCIAL

Adapted from John Holland, *Making Vocational Choices: A Theory of Careers*, pp. 14-18.

Describing Your World

Holland has also developed descriptions of six main types of work environments. It will be useful to look at their primary characteristics and what effects these environments have on the individuals involved in them. (Do not let the distinction between working for pay and working at home get in your way. We are talking here about the places people spend most of their active time.) You will, as you read, want to watch for the categories that best describe the basic housework job description, as well as the many ways "homemaking" expands it.

The Realistic environment fosters technical competencies and achievements and stimulates people to perform realistic activities such as using tools and machines. (Home examples include mops and vacuums, ovens and washers.) This environment encourages people to see the world in simple, tangible, and traditional terms, and it rewards them when they value the conventional money, power, and possessions.

The Conventional environment in the working world most often includes record keeping, filing, typing, and organizing numerical data. "It encourages people to see themselves as conforming, orderly, non-artistic and to see the world in conventional, stereotyped, constricted, simple, and dependent ways. It rewards people when they value money, dependability, and conformity." This description, though taken from Holland's research (*Making Vocational Choices,* p. 33) seems to be right out of the pages of *The Feminine Mystique,* describing the 1950s' housewife. (Home examples might include planning the week's menus on file cards, grocery shopping every Wednesday at nine, and keeping the records for the babysitting co-op.)

Holland goes on to describe the other four work environments, but the key question in responding to depression is: What happens to the woman who is in fact a person whose essential self is not primarily Realistic or Conventional? How does she cope with the housewife role? I would argue that this "miscasting" contributes in a major way to her depression.

The alternative is to seek out more creative opportunities. The Social housewife finds any excuse to leave her housework to talk on the phone or to visit a friend. Or she may be, in fact if not in name, a kitchen counselor. To be away from people and human interaction causes her to feel bound up and depressed from lack of stimulation.

The Investigative woman working at home may find herself taking apart the vacuum to see why it will not work. She may be an insatiable reader. If her curious analytical side does not find satisfying outlets, her passive and pessimistic side can feed her depression.

The Enterprising woman is not limited to economic endeavors. She thrives on responsibility and leadership opportunities. She may find herself developing a "serendipity fair" for her church one Saturday in May. Though she's nervous, she is still secretly delighted to be asked to speak to the League of Women Voters' special convocation in her city. She may begin to see clues as to what causes her depression if it only occurs between these "high" activities in the slump when all she has to look forward to are cleaning and changing beds. Or her stimulating activities may, by pumping adrenalin, be overriding a mild chemical depression.

In order to fully bloom and flower, both the Social and Enterprising talents may require settings where achievement is a primary value. But it is difficult for many women to give themselves permission to achieve. As Rachael Conrad Wahlberg points out in *Jesus According to a Woman*, " . . . boys and men learn that to be achievers is right and expected of them, (while) girls and women learn that to achieve in a vocational sense is somehow regarded as selfish. *Their* obligation is to serve the family" [p. 85]. The point here is not that families are not to be served. The point is that women are given gifts and talents in areas of endeavor that may inevitably be achievement-oriented, and these women are denying God's gifts when they discount achievement from their self-concept and their future.

The Artistic housewife frequently chafes at the day-to-day routines required by her job. She'd rather be painting (canvas or walls) or writing. She may clean her house with a different system each time . . . because she's usually building a bookshelf or putting up wallpaper instead. The talents push toward the surface. When they go unacknowledged and unchanneled, she may become a compulsive doer; the gifts refuse to be totally ignored.

A word should be said here about the concept of "artistic" people and creativity. I have heard many, many women say, "I'm not creative." They usually mean, "When I try to draw a horse, it never looks like it should," or "I can't knit." These images of creativity are inadequate. The Artistic category, for both job type and personality, is much more expansive and liberating. Creativity also means:

- thinking new thoughts, being open to new possibilities
- seeking new solutions to old problems
- improvising ideas or solutions on the spur of the moment
- enjoying not doing the same thing twice, but preferring to introduce variety into even the most mundane tasks
- anticipating needs, showing foresight
- and much, much more.

Nearly everyone has more of a creative sense than they've let out of their box. Leave the lid off now and then and see what pops out.

If role dissatisfaction seems to be part of your depression, see how far away from the Realistic/Conventional sections of the hexagon your own truest self lies. If you discover you are primarily artistic, you shouldn't be surprised that the traditional homemaking tasks are not fully rewarding for you. The debate still rages about whether homemaking "ought to be" fulfilling for women. The Holland career model refreshingly suggests to me a way to cut across sex and role categories and ask, "What are your primary talents and interests? Do they make sense in this job?"

The next question, then, is, "How do you find the 'right job'?" Once you have some inkling of what type of person you are, and which types of environments and activities bring out your best, you have the opportunity to examine your priorities. How much time do you want to spend developing this newfound area? How much flexibility do you have to do so? Can you get help with cleaning, for example, to keep the

Realistic jobs to a minimum, so you can take up real estate sales, pot throwing, or do-your-own income tax courses? Is it worth it to do sewing for someone if she'll do cleaning for you? If you are primarily a social being, how will you arrange to get out of the house to interact with others? Or will you enterprisingly design a way to get people to come to you?

Don't be bound by existing job categories. Use the ideas to stimulate your own inventiveness. Ask yourself, and brainstorm with friends, how you can best be social or enterprising, artistic or investigative, or even realistic and conventional in new and rewarding ways?

Actual people are more complex than our illustrations. Jobs seldom fall into clearcut "social" or "realistic" molds. To help overcome this problem of oversimplification, Holland suggests that people be described by their three strongest areas, in a cluster of interests. The journalist, for example, may be Artistic-Social-Enterprising. At the end of this chapter some career tests are described that can provide you with systematic tools for finding yourself and your interests in more depth. They will give you fairly precise readings on which types on the hexagon you are and which are most unlike you.

Taking Action

Richard Bolles has revolutionized the career planning/job hunting field by asking, "What job or career is most suited to your unique capabilities?" instead of the traditional question, "What job can you get?" The old way put the searcher at the mercy of the market and the employer's whims; and she somewhat passively bounced from want ad to interview. The new approach means taking charge of your destiny, seeking out or creating the job that most nearly suits your unique needs and talents.

You, the housewife, are faced with the same alternative. You can passively accept the job description someone else (who knows where or when?) thought up. Or you can take charge of your destiny and individually mold your activities to suit the type of person you are. Will you choose to let it happen, or will you make it happen? Here are some action steps for making it happen:

1. Look at your lifeline graph. Begin to answer the question, where do you go from here? You might ask, for example, where might further education fit in? When will all those babies be in school? How will your options change as children grow older? How will their changes affect your time? your available money? When will your children all move away? How many different options will retirement bring? And perhaps the hardest question to face, how do you want to prepare yourself for the possibilities that (a) you might have to support yourself unexpectedly and (b) you will very likely outlive your husband in any case?

2. Identify what stage of life you are now in and seek further insights on how this might be influencing your depression. Record your learnings in your journal. Studies of *clinically* depressed middle-aged women, for example, indicate that significantly higher psychiatric symptoms scores occurred with women not employed outside the home. Meaningful employment (or volunteer work with an equal degree of commitment) apparently provides not only feelings of self-worth and accomplishment but also generally protective psychological effects.

3. Experiment and get feedback. Try the following five processes, in any order and to whatever degree works for you:

● Try things. Just sitting and imagining what it would be like will not tell you how you *really* like doing something. Go for a hike, needlepoint your first pillow, take "beginning ballet for the overweight," chair a committee, campaign against nuclear weapons, or take in college boarders. Only doing it will tell you what you need to know. You'll fear failure. Everyone does. Do it anyway.

● Get comments from the people around you—the ballet teacher, the committee member, the college students. It takes nerve to ask, "How am I doing?" But no matter what the response, you learn something. One word of caution: Many women experimenting with new ideas and activities have found that their husbands are not their best fans. Your growth may be threatening to him at first. If his standard reply is, "Why would you want to go and do *that*?" you'll want to seek encouragement elsewhere until your confidence is built up. Chances are by then he'll be bragging at the office about your new skills and adventures.

- Career testing and guidance: You need not be planning to go to work for a salary in order to benefit from a thorough analysis of your skills and interests. Most community colleges have counseling departments that will process your tests for a modest fee. They have a barrage of no-wrong-answer tests you can take, and the guidance counselor will help you interpret your results.

- If you are working through this book with a small group, ask these friends for their invaluable comments. If they point out skills or talents you do not rate highly in yourself, listen to them more carefully! They probably see a side of you that you've not yet fully recognized.

- Keep an active dialogue going in your journal. Record all your insights from the above steps and from the books you're reading. You can create a special journal section on "life planning" or "gifts and talents search." Reflect during quiet times on the meanings and implications of what you've written. Over the months, or years, the movement and new insights you experience will begin to show progressive patterns as you read back over the previous entries. Your journal provides the map for your journey, indicating both where you've been and where you might choose to go in the future.

Browsing through a *National Geographic* one day in a doctor's waiting room, I noticed a remarkable aerial photograph of a vast desert. A highway bisected the picture, and in the center was a large C-shaped detour. The jog in the road was built because the sand dunes had at one point entirely covered the original highway. There was, apparently, no expectation of bulldozing the sand off the road, as one would remove drifted snow. I could see it was only a matter of time before a larger "C" would be built, when the sand overtook the first detour.

Your gifts and talents are the original highway, covered over by sand since before you can remember. The first seven chapters in this book have provided some excellent detours and coping mechanisms. With this chapter you've begun the "digging out." You're beginning to take charge of who you are and what you will become. Your original highway is beginning to be uncovered. As you move into Chapter 9, you will learn more and more of what it means to drive a straight path into your own special future.

Suggested Assignments

1. Write out your own short autobiography of the "stage" you are now in. If you're in a group, discussing these at your next meeting will be helpful. Be as specific as possible, such as, "I have nine and a half more years of childraising," or "I have fourteen years until Fred retires, but I have thirty-two more years for my 'career,' unless I outlive the statistics."

2. A number of helpful and revealing tests are now available to help you "find yourself on the hexagon." The counseling center at your community college (or high school) can be a likely place to inquire. Ask them if you can take, for example:

   a. The Self-Directed Search, by John Holland. This test, which you score yourself, gives you numerical scores in the six areas. You also get a coded "Occupations Finder" that lists about 500 occupations, telling you which jobs are primarily realistic, social, etc. The cost is quite reasonable.

   b. The Strong-Campbell Interest Inventory lets you compare your preferences with those of successful people in a wide range of occupations. You might, for example, find you have a score of fifty-two sharing interests with an advertising executive, and a six with a research physicist. Again (as with the Self-Directed Search) you receive numerical weights showing your preferences for Holland's six types. This test must be scored by a computer, and the test fee may include a useful conference with the college's counselor to help you interpret your scores.

c. Another approach to the hexagon test is found in Richard Bolles' book *The Quick Job-Hunting Map,* available at your bookstore or from Ten Speed Press, Box 7123, Berkeley, Calif. 94707. This test asks you to recreate on paper seven accomplishments or experiences in your life; you're then guided to identify the skills, competencies, and interests you've exhibited.

I recommend taking all three of the above-mentioned tests, with the Bolles coming first because it gives you a feel for *what* in your past has led to who you are.

Suggested Readings

Richard N. Bolles, *The Quick Job-Hunting Map.* Berkeley: Ten Speed Press, 1979.

Iris Sanguiliano, *In Her Time.* New York: Morrow Quill Paperbacks, 1980. A highly readable reflection on women finding their identities and life directions.

Richard N. Bolles, *What Color Is Your Parachute?* Berkeley: Ten Speed Press, 1981. See Chapter 5, "Only *You* Can Decide: What Do You Want to Do?"

John Holland, *Making Vocational Choices: A Theory of Careers.* Englewood Cliffs, N.J.: Prentice-Hall, 1973.

Rachael Conrad Wahlberg, *Jesus According to a Woman.* New York: Paulist Press, 1975.

9

Taking Charge

Billie Jean King says tennis is 90% psych. I think life is 90% psych. It's how you think about where you're headed that makes the difference. Tennis offers a good lesson for approaching life and overcoming depression. I am only a casual, on-and-off tennis player, but I've isolated the factor that almost always determines if I win or lose: body attitude. This, in turn, is derived from head attitude. If I am feeling "up" when I go onto the court, if I'm on my toes, leaning forward, ready to step out into every play, I usually win. If I approach the day feeling as if my weight is back on my heels, if I'm letting things happen *to* me, I lose. Winning seems to require a certain dose of aggressive spirit to stay "on top of the ball." When I feel more passive, I run after the ball, but I'm always a split second too late and too weak to return it well.

What a strong parallel to depression fighting! This chapter is all about how to live "forward on your toes" in your whole approach to life. The thesis of the chapter is that depression will be conquered only when you take charge of your feelings, your actions, and your future. The fact is, you'll not be able to put to effective use the other chapters in this book unless you take charge of your own life.

The Passive Stance

How do women seem to fall naturally into the passive/reactive stance? A whole cluster of forces are at work both in the social environment and in women's heads. They are helplessness, dependence, blaming, a sense of powerlessness, and insufficient rewards, recognition, and satisfactions. All these forces can be frequent causes of depression. The "taking charge stance" is crucial to counteracting these forces and thereby preventing or getting rid of depression.

Women have traditionally been economically dependent upon their husbands; the wives may never have worked, or have worked only at low-paying jobs. They often grew up assuming that the important decisions for their lives would be made by men. It has, therefore, never occurred to these women that they might take primary responsibility for their own lives. Various social forces reinforce this assumed sense of powerlessness. Traditionally, if a woman married early in life, she would go directly from her parents' home to the home of her husband. If she considered a career, it was thought of as what she'd do "until" marriage.

The cultural environment has taught women a distinct brand of adult helplessness. It's easy for a woman to assume that her contribution doesn't matter when, no matter what she does, nothing ever changes. If she constantly picks up toys and clothes, but the house continues to be messy, she can easily conclude that she is helpless to really change anything. It's not so much a matter of whether she is or is not in fact helpless. It's mostly "psych," that is, how many things she *perceives* she is able or unable to control. As often happens with the accompanying depression, she overgeneralizes from the circumstances she's experienced so far that she'll always be helpless to affect her world. Her spontaneous motivation disappears when she feels locked in, and she gives up. This is missing one serve and letting the next three go by.

The development of the gifts and talents discussed in Chapter 8 is also affected by this powerlessness mentality. Woman has heard for centuries that developing her potential and capacities is less important than man's developing his, *and* that her development must not be allowed to interfere with his. Women have responded by seeking favor from the men who ran things by trying to please them, by trying to tie their interests to their husbands' and go along for that ride, or by whatever other means they could come up with. In some quarters today these assumptions are still held and women are still less valued than men, even in their developed form.

The mindset operating here is one of dependence and deference. Women assume so readily that they are dependent on men that it may not even occur to them it can be any other way. Interdependence is still a very new word for most women. In a mixed group they often let the men set the tone of the conversation; in a committee they may look to a man to chair it; if a woman is suggested as chair, her first thought may be that she's not as capable as Mr. X.

Women have been trained by our culture to take a back seat, to *re*act to needs rather than to act, to let someone else take final responsibility for how women feel, think, and act, rather than take that responsibility themselves. In a situation as simple as opening a casual conversation, a woman will often wait to gauge the other's actions and edit her own response to what she thinks the other expects. It never occurs to her to initiate the dialogue and set the tone herself for the interchange.

In *Self-Assertion for Women,* Dr. Pamela Butler highlights this dilemma by asking several key questions:

> How can a woman express anger, an emotion deriving from the frustration of her own needs, when her role is to nurture other people? How does a woman say "no" to another person's request when she has been taught to live *for* that other person? How can she initiate an action that derives from her own sense of what she wants to accomplish when she has been instructed to receive her satisfactions *through* the accomplishments of someone else? Why does she need to look at her own talents and potentials when another tenant of her sex role instructs her to rely on a male provider for sustenance and status? (p. 7)

This mindset precludes the human quality of self-reliance from being part of the "proper" feminine experience. It pushes all women into a role that is less than fully human.

Richard Bolles, in *The Three Boxes of Life,* describes this deference phenomenon by calling it the Victim Mentality— an attitude toward life in which persons assume that forces beyond them control their lives. With women at home the powerful "they" forces often include husbands and children. "If it weren't for Jack, I could. . . ." Or, "If I didn't have to . . . , I could. . . ." It's true, of course, that none of us is entirely free to do as we wish, but as Bolles points out, every one of us has more personal freedom, more opportunity, more choices than we realize.

Bolles is really talking about blaming. Unfortunately for the vast number of women who follow this pattern, the blaming mentality is a trap. It's self-defeating; and it's depressing. If a woman blames herself for all her problems, she is probably worse off, because she must build up her self-image before she'll *believe* she has the power to take charge of her feelings and her situation. Hopelessness is most threatening. The woman who blames other people or outside circumstances still has much work to do, even though she has taken the self-blame monkey off her back. The problem with blaming is that she tends to wait for someone or something to "fix it." And the fact is, no one out there cares nearly as much about fixing the problem as she does. When powerlessness is a cause of depression, it's not a matter of how powerful a woman actually is nor of how much real control she has over her destiny. What triggers depression for her is the *feeling* she experiences of having little control over her life. For her, taking a more active role in how life turns out each day is the essential step in putting depression behind her. If she decides to take charge, she begins to get more positive strokes. Insufficient rewards, lack of recognition, and too little satisfaction all contribute to depression. The more active a stance she takes toward life, the more rewards she'll experience. Behaviorists call it more positive reinforcement, and taking charge increases its return.

Taking Charge of Your Feelings

I said to Sue Ann and the group one day, "Taking charge of your own life can be broken down into three areas: taking responsibility for your feelings, your actions, and your destiny." How we feel is something most of us imagine we have little control over. Circumstances happen all around us, and we respond with feelings like an automatic cause and effect, or so it seems. Viktor Frankl shows us in *Man's Search for*

Meaning that circumstances do not necessarily need to control our feelings. In fact, we have control over our attitudes when everything around us is controlled by others. The book recounts his experiences living in a World War II concentration camp; many readers have concluded that it was Frankl's positive attitude that saved him, while others all around him died in the terrible conditions. His life story powerfully demonstrates that we *can* control and choose our feelings. I find it very encouraging to know that a person found this personal power in the most grim of human circumstances. It means there is undeniable hope for me, a relatively comfortable suburbanite, to find such power over my feelings. Chapter 7 deals with the Cognitive Therapy approach and merits reviewing when you've completed this chapter.

The types of feelings we might experience are, of course, quite numerous. If we list feelings associated with joy and elation, and then list those that have to do with down feelings or depression, we can observe a curious pattern. Notice how many of the "joy" words reflect a positive "I am" stance, where the "down" words express a passive "done to me" quality, as if someone else is allowed to be in control of how you feel.

Some joy and elation words

blissful	fit	proud
calm	glad	satisfied
cheerful	glorious	serene
comical	happy	thrilled
delighted	humorous	triumphant
ecstatic	jovial	vivacious
enthusiastic	jubilant	witty
excited	overjoyed	wonderful
fine	pleasant	

Some down-feeling words

abandoned	downtrodden	rebuked
alienated	estranged	rejected
alone	excluded	run down
battered	forsaken	sad
blue	grim	stranded

cast off	hated	tearful
crushed	hopeless	unhappy
defeated	humiliated	unloved
degraded	hurt	whipped
dejected	left out	worthless
dismal	overlooked	wrecked

Studies by psychologists Carl Rogers, Richard Crutchfield, and others indicate that people who see themselves and their situation clearly and who freely take responsibility for that self and situation are very different from those who feel controlled by outside circumstances. The former persons cope more successfully with pressures and stress; they are more open, free, and spontaneous. Most important, the changes and growth they seek only become possible when they reach the point of saying, "I am someone. I am worth something, a valuable, important being. I am committed to making changes and pushing for growth."

Taking responsibility for your feelings may mean deciding you are not going to let a sudden disappointment get you down. With practice you can come to recognize immediately the empty feeling in your stomach when an activity you'd been counting on fails to materialize. You can train yourself to notice the black clouds forming on your emotional horizon. Before the depression hits, you can say to yourself, "This time it's going to be different."

Expectations are another category of feelings that can greatly influence depression. The good news is that we can have complete control over our expectations. If we spend much time longing for what may never be, we set ourselves up for continual disappointment and depression. Joann wished the kids wouldn't scream . . . ever. Susan had the dream of keeping her house "Better Homes" sparkling, even though she hated housework and had no interest in spending time at it. I call these particular expectations the "wishing for the housefairy to come" approach. Housefairies don't come very often. Expecting that they ought to come to save you sets you up for depression when the mess remains.

A special word should be said about husbands and expectations. Some women would argue that husbands are a major cause of depression in wives. "If only he would be more loving, more considerate, more helpful around the house, more appreciative, more encouraging. . . ." The list goes on. The problem with wishing a Prince Charming would come through the door, when it's always just old Fred, is that you set yourself up for disappointment. Even expecting your husband to change in some very reasonable ways, or to begin to act in ways any considerate human being ought to act, sets you up for the whole array of sad feelings when it doesn't come about.

Perfect spouses are rare. If you don't believe it, ask yourself if you are one of them. Most of us have to learn practical ways to come to terms with a less-than-perfect spouse. Lynn was in her eighteenth year of marriage before she realized that she couldn't change her husband. When she finally came to terms with two realities, she discovered a new sense of freedom. "I can't *make* him change, because it doesn't work. But if I sit around and *wait* for him to change, I'm dead. The only thing for me to do is work on *my* side. Now I look for other sources to meet some of my needs. And I work a little harder at seeing that I'm a good partner." Lynn had made a crucial discovery. Her expectations of her husband could be depressing if she let them be. She decided to take responsibility for her own side, her own feelings, her own life, to make the best of what she could change.

It's a trap to allow other people's actions toward you (or their failure to act) determine how you feel inside. You might call it "the tyranny of great expectations." You have the power, you have the choice, to examine what your expectations have been, and then to alter them, or even to set them all aside until you have a better handle on your feelings.

Taking Charge of Your Actions

The housewives' group discovered an important bit of reality while they were experimenting with taking charge of their feelings and expectations. At some point, they found, they needed to mix action with working on positive feelings. Much of the emphasis in the preceding chapters has been on doing things. Simply deciding you will, in fact, *do* them is part of taking responsibility for how your life will proceed.

Choosing actions that can make you feel better means discovering and developing a long list of what brings satisfaction in your life. You might set up a program by spelling out in your journal those actions and activities from the previous chapters that best serve your individual needs. When Jayne had done this for several weeks, she reported a new sense of power and a lot more energy. "It feels great to seize an opportunity and *do* it!"

One avenue guaranteed to bring positive rewards is exploring the growing field of assertiveness training. While the title puts some people off ("I don't want to learn to be aggressive"), properly understood, assertiveness is a way of enhancing your God-given personhood. Dr. Pamela Butler, in *Self-Assertion for Women*, offers numerous and pointed examples that help the reader get in touch with real-life circumstances. Through the author's guidance, the reader can begin to imagine and finally practice the skills of being more fully her own person. Assertiveness training is, I told the group one day, as essential today as learning to drive. You're just too helpless without it.

Risking is another part of acting responsibly with your own life. It's an unavoidable part of becoming the personally powerful person you were created to be. Risking means deliberately putting yourself into new situations where you must test new skills, strengthen new "muscles." You must seek actions through which you can change and stretch to the next step in your growth. Later you can reflect on the situation and gather meanings and new insights. But you cannot simply do the reflecting without the doing and risking.

One of the risks most difficult for women to imagine as they seek new stances of personal responsibility is the risk of making mistakes. Everyone likes to feel, going into a situation, that they'll do okay, or even that they'll succeed marvelously. Many of us, though, have learned that the way to avoid making mistakes is to avoid doing anything new or risky. In *Games Your Mother Never Taught You*, Betty Lehan Harragan tries to show women that it's okay to make mistakes. If you take charge of something new, and you do make some mistakes, you learn far more about yourself and the situation than you would if everything went smoothly. Some think the goal is to never make mistakes; the real secret is to always learn from them. The golden ideal is, perhaps, to never make the same mistake twice. Be willing to keep making new ones and learning from them.

Ask yourself, "Do I really believe I'm free to fail? What's so serious if I do fail? Can I live with the consequences of what may transpire? What are the worst things that can happen? Do I want this experience for myself right now, regardless?" Your answers will nearly always provide far less than disastrous possibilities. If you're worried about venturing out—a phone call to a stranger, chairing a committee—this brief rundown of the consequences often yields possibilities like, "They won't like me"; "They might be mad at me"; "They'll think I'm stupid (awkward, clumsy)." Taking charge means taking risks that are worth it.

Your journal can be a great ally if you still have cold feet. Describe doing the risky activity in writing. Then relate it out loud to your group or to a supportive friend. These two "rehearsals" take the sting out. By running it clearly through your imagination in these ways to see how it feels, you find out it's not all that bad. When you finally do the action for real, it's "the second or third time around" and comes much more easily.

Joan knew she would have to start taking some specific action if she was to get beyond her many "gray days." When a friend asked her if they might set up a babysitting arrangement, trading on Tuesdays and Thursdays after preschool, Joan's first response was to turn down the offer. She'd never done it before and the whole idea felt threatening. But she asked for a week to think about it and realized this was as good a beginning as any. She decided she would have to intentionally think up activities that would draw her out of the house, even if they seemed risky. She remembered she wanted to learn to play tennis "someday." Why not sign up for lessons now? She'd wanted to refinish an old chest, but it had been sitting in the garage for two years because she'd not known quite how to go about doing it. By the end of the week she called her friend and set up the trading arrangement. She found a short course at a furniture shop and tackled the chest. Tennis proved to be a delightfully vigorous outing each week. By the end of the third week, more opportunities had come to her attention than she had time for. She tutored reading at the neighborhood school. Much to her surprise, her two young students blossomed in her presence as the weeks went on. She had risked "not knowing what to do" and was rewarded.

Joan's decision to risk the unfamiliar and her subsequent commitment to action illustrates an important principle. There is power in the very act of making a commitment. It has been said that the moment a person definitely commits herself, Providence moves too. All sorts of things happen to help the project that otherwise would never have occurred. Unforeseen incidents and meetings rise in her path to aid. Goethe puts it well:

Whatever you can do, or dream you can, begin it.
Boldness has genius, power and magic in it. *(Faust)*

Making decisions is part of being human. Making more and more daring decisions, acting more boldly, is part of becoming more fully a woman created in God's image.

One final observation on taking action. Be constantly aware of whatever resistance is operating on any given day. Excuses are easy to come by. There always seems to be a handy reason not to take charge.

Taking Charge of Your Future

At the outset it's important to acknowledge that none of us entirely controls our future, but we *can* choose to take an active or a passive stance toward influencing our future.

Chapter 8 on gifts and life planning focuses on your developing future. By consciously making choices in the direction of your unique talents, you can seek out and affirm the best possible life you were meant to live. An underlying assumption in Chapter 8 is that you can affirmatively choose new directions in which to spend your energies and your time.

To fail to do so is to be tossed to and fro by the winds of others' demands and expectations or, worse, to live in a partial vacuum with no direction or focus. The passive "back on your heels" stance for life planning is not planning at all. You can miss the ball and lose the match by letting life happen to you this way. Deciding on the active stance over the long haul, as well as day by day, is the first step to moving into your future.

As you think about where you are going with your life, and how you will get there, beware of an assumption that lies at the very heart of our culture today: that people, especially women, need to "adjust" to the world around them. The expectation is that if the person can adjust and fit nicely with the way things are, he or she will be satisfied and happy. If the person and the society don't entirely "fit," the blame is on the individual for being "maladjusted." Presumably the person needs to "shape up." The catch is that we unconsciously assume nothing is amiss in the environment or the social system in which the individual is trying to live. In an imperfect world, we dare not make that assumption.

The behavioral norms and established assumptions for women are being seriously challenged today, with much benefit. Many God-given talents and gifts are now being discovered and used, and undirected energies are finally being unleashed. Formulate your own fresh assumptions about how things "must" be as one way to help free yourself for a different future. Dr. Pamela Butler presents an excellent illustration of the whole woman, showing how expectations for her have allowed only half of her personality to live and thrive. In *Self-Assertion for Women,* Dr. Butler says: "The stereotypic feminine woman in our society is taught to express certain desirable characteristics and to inhibit others. In one sense, she is allowed to assert half of who she is as a complete human being." According to Butler's diagram, the stereotypic woman is encouraged to be "nurturing, affectionate, cheerful, gullible, yielding, childlike, flatterable, dependent, and sensitive." She is told *not* to be "objective, adventurous, powerful, analytical, ambitious, aggressive, dominant, competitive, or self-sufficient" (p. 8).

In your long-range thinking you'll want to encourage expression of your whole self, in order to become the full person you can be. It's harder to change your world and yourself than it is to sit back and "let it happen," but it's infinitely more rewarding.

When this book was nearly completed, Carolyn's husband received word he was to be transferred to the Far East. The news sent her reeling, but she soon realized she had a choice. She could either let the situation throw her future life into chaos and perhaps depression, or she could take hold and make it into a positive experience. She chose to take charge.

She dealt with her feelings first. Her immediate responses were many: fear and apprehension at the strange and foreign place she was supposed to live in; resentment that The Company would dare disrupt her life so completely; powerlessness, an immediate sense of having no say in the matter; loss of friends, of roots, of familiar things, of snowy winters and a dog and a cat, of a just-blooming Outward Bound project. Carolyn realized that she had the power to experience many different feelings about her situation. She did not have to be fearful. By researching and asking innumerable questions about the new area, she could eliminate much of the unknown. Though there would certainly be much loss, which she chose to mourn and then move beyond, she began a list of the beckoning new experiences this foreign world would bring. She decided to welcome the adventure! Her resentment and powerless feelings were diffused when she realized she actually had many choices. She could, if she decided to, simply not go. It was not an impossible option to stay in the house until her husband returned, just as sea captains' wives had done for centuries; she could choose to return after a year to spend summers at home; her husband could quit and find another job, and so on. As her list of possible alternatives increased, her sense of powerlessness decreased significantly.

Carolyn began to take action with a new enthusiasm, once she made her *own* affirmative *choice* to go. She took specific steps to create a positive experience: learning all she could about the new place, writing to people already living there, seeking out people who had lived there in the past, planning the move in careful detail, choosing thoughtfully what to take and what to leave behind, and preparing her son for the many changes he would face. She arranged meaningful goodbyes as the departure date drew close. She kept track of feelings and actions in her journal and planned a whole arsenal of survival methods to ward off depression once she arrived. Her friends from the group gave her as a going-away present a stack of bound blank books for future journal volumes.

Carolyn's long-range planning included repeatedly asking herself the question, "What marvelous things can I make of this unusual experience?" and "How can I make this segment of my lifetime a positive and unique growth time?" She realized in her reflections that she might well have been saying to herself, "I'll be stuck here for five years, and life will finally resume when I get back home."

Months later, she wrote back to the housewives' group:

> I could never have survived the uprooting, the culture shock, the incredible adjustments, without all I learned from the group in our time together. Often I see situations which could easily bring on depression. But I am confident in my knowledge that God has bigger hopes for me and that I can actively pursue a positive, creative life here on the other side of the world. Taking hold of my life and really *living* it has made all the difference. Thank you for being such an important part of my growth.

The Role of Support Groups in Taking Charge

Carolyn's story highlights an important principle in the whole process of taking charge to banish depression: A support group is invaluable. Some of the circumstances you face as you seek to overcome depression will—despite all your efforts to be realistic, take charge, and remain hopeful—persist as seemingly immovable blocks to your progress. Others will just nag at you, not seeming to be important enough to feel strongly about, but remaining unresolved. Not all the answers will come as easily as painting the kitchen yellow or taking a brisk walk. Some problems will be impossible to ignore, like a husband who remains steadfastly threatened by signs of your growing potential for achievement outside the home, or the determined efforts in your church to hammer home theological arguments to "keep women in the place God intended for them." Going it alone is not the best way. Until you have experienced the remarkable support of other women who genuinely care for your growth and your welfare, you cannot imagine how encouraging and stimulating this resource can be and how it can actually help you take charge.

The "American way" seems to have taught us to say, "I ought to be able to handle this alone" or "I'm probably the only one with this problem." As Chapter 3 noted, we have been taught to be isolated rather than supportive, competitive rather than cooperative. But women can *decide* to hold different values. They can choose to support one another through difficult changes, rather than go it alone.

Group discussions can help women take charge: to see there are many forces at work "out there" that threaten but that *can* be overcome; to discover how frequently women nevertheless tend to turn their aggression and blame inward. Women learn to give each other courage to achieve personal power and responsibility over their circumstances.

The group process can also foster responsibility by being structured as a leaderless or shared-leadership group. Each woman is recognized as an authority on her own experience. Each woman's judgment as to what path she must take at any given point is honored and supported. The group norms listed in Part Four, Section B (how to lead a support group) are designed to enhance this process.

As members of the group come to their own "ah-ha" experiences, that is, glimpsing personal responsibility in new and specific ways, their sharing of the stories helps the others see more clearly and move more boldly. Such dynamics are impossible when a woman tries to go it alone. As we've noted earlier, the point of greatest potential for growth and change is the place where a woman realizes, "I'm not the only one. You, too, are there, or you've been along this path. You have changed, and so can I."

Women who have tried individual psychotherapy point out noticeable contrasts with being in a support group. In therapy it is *the professional* who gets the practice and enjoys the benefits of the dynamics:

- taking the initiative and feeling the surge of energy that comes with it
- taking responsibility for what's going on and reaping its rewards if he/she is successful
- setting up a productive program and seeing someone through it.

In a support group the women themselves can collect these bonuses.

There are at least five essential factors to successful support groups that will foster the kind of personal power and responsibility this chapter advocates.

1. *Peer equality.* There should be no authority figure in the group to "give answers," especially a male. I am not against men or experts. I am not against highly trained people who bring information and needed guidance to those who are searching. My concern here is with women who, out of habit, mindlessly give themselves over to whatever falls from the lips of an expert or from any man in a group. I am against a woman unquestioningly relinquishing the power over and the responsibility for her own life in the face of someone who "must know" what is good for her. There is room in the small group for informed resource people, whose valuable information the members can weigh with their own judgment, but women need to examine more carefully the awe they hold for the experts all around them.

2. *Sisterhood.* Too many women have been trained in the past not to trust other women. They sometimes prefer confiding in a trusted man friend and see other women either as uninformed, competitive, or in any case, as persons with whom secrets cannot be shared. Or, perhaps more commonly, a woman may trust her closest woman friend but write off most other women. A support group may be the first setting wherein you learn to trust and work closely with other women without suspicion or labels imposed by the culture. An intimate and growth-fostering atmosphere becomes possible when the other

women are not judged or dismissed because they are "dumpy," or "too pretty," "sexy," or "dumb." Women in these groups are often surprised at the value and esteem they discover in their newfound sisters. Decreasing one's prejudice regarding other women is an important step in personal power. Women can learn something that's eluded many men: we can gain power without needing to put others down.

3. *Self-help.* Nothing beats a good self-help group for getting rid of depression and specifically for developing personal responsibility for one's life. John Drakeford has written an excellent book, *People to People Therapy,* which spells out in detail not only the value but the how-to principles of mutual self-help groups.

4. *Action.* A well-run (group-run) support group will make a point to intentionally motivate the members to act on and solve problems, not just talk about them. Personal responsibility is built *only* by practicing it, not by talking about how it ought to happen . . . someday soon.

5. *Personal responsibility.* Each group must walk the fine line of support without taking over responsibility for the individual. There is a paradox in group-fostered personal responsibility that must be gingerly respected. Just as expert interpretations imposed with no chance to dispute them bring a serious threat to personal power, so, too, group pressure and group opinion can jeopardize that power. The group must reverently respect the individual's self-assessment, personally reasoned and intuitive appraisals of her own needs and solutions. Only in this way can she learn what it truly means to take full responsibility for her own feelings and actions.

Suggested Assignments

1. Begin collecting your own checklist of:
   - The early-warning signs of depression
   - What triggers it for you
   - What you will *do* when you detect these early warning signals.

You have the power to control your depression only to the extent of your awareness of the power you have given it over you.

2. Discuss in your journal or in your group how you feel about this statement:

> As a daughter of my time and place I had never been taught to function as a total, independent being, and the prospect of assuming full responsibility for a life in which there weren't even any positive guidelines, structures, or traditions terrified me, left me helpless. (*The Prime of Ms. America: The American Woman at Forty,* Janet Harris [New York: G.P. Putnam's Sons, 1975, p. 217])

3. Reflect in your journal: Who or what do you feel has the greatest power over you? Then, begin a list of where you could (or do) feel some free or partial choice, or at least some limited control over the situation. (Eventually this latter list should grow long.)

4. Select three or four areas for which you want to take more responsibility. Begin working on them one at a time. For example, "The next time I go to the doctor, I'll remember my health is primarily *my* responsibility. I'll not expect magic pills to fix me when I've not been willing to take sensible care of myself. Also, I'll ask all the 'dumb' questions."

   Afterward, answer these questions in your journal: How did you feel? What happened? Was it bad? (Scary? Worrisome? Threatening?) Was it as bad as you'd feared? What did you learn about yourself in doing it? What were the rewards? Are you changed in any way?

   When you feel you can do so honestly, complete this sentence in your journal: I have now begun to take charge of the _____ area of my life.

5. One housewife said, "I keep reading these books. Why isn't anything happening?" If you've been simply reading this book but not acting so far, now is the time to choose the chapter that most speaks to your situation and start doing something new with your life.

Suggested Readings

Pamela Butler, *Self-Assertion for Women*. San Francisco: Harper & Row, 1976. Based on the assertiveness classes Dr. Butler has taught, this is a most useful book for learning to take charge of your life.

Madonna Kolbenschlag, *Kiss Sleeping Beauty Good-Bye*. New York: Bantam Books, 1981. Subtitled "Breaking the Spell of Feminine Myths and Models," the book dismantles many assumptions women have unconsciously leaned on.

Helen DeRosis and Victoria Pellegrino, *The Book of Hope*. New York: Macmillan, 1976. If your expectations give you special problems, this book may prove particularly helpful.

Richard N. Bolles, *The Three Boxes of Life, and How to Get Out of Them*. Berkeley: Ten Speed Press, 1978.

Betty Friedan, *The Feminine Mystique*. Chapter 8.

John Drakeford, *People to People Therapy: Self-help Groups— Root Principles and Processes*. New York: Harper & Row, 1978. Drakeford gives an excellent outline of what it takes to make a good group "work." Worth owning if you hope to organize a housewives' depression self-help group.

Viktor Frankl's *Man's Search for Meaning* is cited at the end of Chapter 10.

10

Finding Purpose in Life

One day Carolyn lingered after the other group members had gone. She spoke weakly of new recipes and a planned wall-paper project. Then, with a hint of anguish in her voice, she asked, "Is this all there is?" I let the question hang in the air, not for dramatic effect, but because I had no quick and easy answer. She groped to restate her dilemma. "There must be more to life than the endless stream of tasks . . . more to life, even, than the long line of creative projects I can think up."

I left her with the question to take home and mull over through the week. I suspected I could not hand her an answer, even if I'd had one.

I did some quick checking that week and discovered that Carolyn was not the only one in the group carrying this question around. She had simply been the first to identify it clearly enough to be able to speak of it. I sought other women not in the group, women who had found their way out of some depres-sion in the past. They confirmed my hunch. I realized I had come upon a final hurdle in overcoming depression: Until you find a purpose in life that you're really sold on and excited about, you cannot overcome depression permanently.

The following week I presented the whole issue of meaning-in-life to the group. They immediately asked, "Well, what are the choices? What might a person's purpose in life *be*?" As the group waded through some fairly new and unexplored questions, we identified at least two ways of coming to an-swers. A first question asks, "What shall I *do* with my life?" The answers to this question come in tangible forms and in the actual trying and doing, day by day. They come from the types of clues generated by Chapter 8. The second level of question asks, "What is the point of my life?" This issue is answered more philosophically and theologically, and perhaps more tentatively. Both questions are subject to change over time; our entire lives are, in a sense, an answering of these questions.

The group began to look at some of the alternatives that presented themselves as answers. We began by recalling the various messages our present culture is sending us concerning our purpose in life. The group noticed immediately that the media does much of the sending. We covered a wall with butcher paper and quickly filled it with lists of the messages we were getting:

- Be the perfect hostess. If you have spotty glasses, you've failed.
- Keep his shirts impeccably clean. If your friends see his ring around the collar, they'll think you're the one who has failed to live up to your potential and purpose in life.
- Make perfect coffee. If he doesn't drink a second cup at home but does when you're out together you've failed again to do what you're supposed to do in life.
- Above all, keep the odors out of your rug. If friends faint when they do pushups on your carpet, you might as well resign from life.
- And when you finally do get out of the house, and you step out of your Mercedes at the theater, be sure you wear a skirt, because gentlemen prefer knees. Never mind what else you have to offer the world, just be sure your legs look great.

The list went on. The group realized that many companies have a great deal to gain by keeping us believing that our only purpose in life is to use their products. Many of the commercial messages devalue the women they are aimed at. Essentially we hear, "You're not a good person, you don't measure up, until you use this product." Several in the group felt it was a depressing experience to be continually bombarded by these kinds of messages, packaged as truth.

John Kenneth Galbraith has been trying for years to alert women to the fact that this society calls us first and foremost to be the "managers of consumption." We're expected not only to continually buy, but to service, fuel, repair, upgrade, and replace the endless line of things we seem to need to live in comfort and ease. I marvel at friends who once capably wielded butcher knives on chopping boards, who now claim they simply cannot prepare a meal without their $200 food processors. Our purpose in life as women-at-home, according to corporate America, is to keep buying at an ever-increasing rate in order to support the growth of the system. No matter that there is no real happiness or deeper purpose to this existence. The unspoken ethic is "whatever is good for our system's growth is good for its people." (We used to hear it as, "What's good for General Motors is good for America.") I watched women like Carolyn beginning to recognize at their very centers that this purpose was hollow, inadequate, and unsatisfying for them, that managing the consumption was not enough reason to get out of bed in the morning.

Aside from the fact that materialism is inherently incapable of deeply satisfying our need for a purpose in life, the "setup" for women-at-home is artificial. Most of what these women "have" they did not earn by their own efforts. Their satisfactions are supposed to come from their husbands' status or accomplishments in the world or from how well their children do in school, on the playing field, and in later life. How these women are regarded, how valuable they are seen to be to the world, is determined largely by others' efforts. Worse yet, those achievements are only marginally under these women's control. The result is often a floating dissatisfaction, elusive to identify because to all outward appearances, they "have everything."

A second purpose for living that women hear today is "service" (also spelled "serve us"). I want to emphasize right from the start that I am not against service as a purpose in life. What I'm against is involuntary servitude. The messages that often bombard women today say: Be Supermom, Be Superhostess, Be Superwife, and even Be Supercareer-while-you-keep-the-house-running-perfectly. Because the unstated corollary is "You're not a good and worthwhile person unless you live out this role to perfection," women too often unconsciously accept these Be Perfect and Serve Us messages in an attempt to feel good about themselves. To voluntarily choose to serve the needs of others is not at all the same as to desperately scurry around from one demand to the next, trying to prove to yourself or to someone else that you're indeed worth something.

The group's discussion of which parts of Supermom and Superwife they each bought into prompted an examination of the term "myth." It is a myth that you can run your house perfectly and that everyone appreciates Mom for all her hard work. It's all a myth because the perfect wife is an unreal image, a composite fiction made up by our society, not something real people ever live up to. We each carry around a whole package of absurd myths. No one can live up to these expectations in the way they're given. And you're no failure if you don't. The myth is a perfect standard the society has constructed out of its wishes and longings, "if only" thoughts, and, of course, economic wants.

The myths must eventually be seen for what they are—simply myths. Just as in Jesus' day people found they could not live up to the Law perfectly, so today women are beginning to realize they cannot live up to the myths of perfection. To try to do so is ultimately self-defeating . . . and impossible. Our purpose and value as human beings are not determined in the trying.

Another way of understanding our culture's answer to purpose in life is to classify it into *having* and *doing*. We are called today to *have:* lovely homes, clean and well-behaved children, a successful husband, a long line of possessions to demonstrate we've arrived at success in life; also talents, honors, education, looks, intelligence, and, of course, youth. Then we are called to the *doing:* be effective, efficient, better than; accomplish, achieve, serve, keep everyone happy. The inadequacy is built in. There's no way to make it all work.

Self-actualization, or the human potential movement, is another common myth about what life is for. The problem lies not in the concept of self-actualization. For women to begin to realize their full potential is great! To learn to become all we are created to be is beautiful. But to make this the entire end in life is disastrous. Self-actualization can become so self-centered it can consume you. When you only look inward you lose all perspective on life. You can lose touch with who you really are.

A hundred other purposes for living have been suggested. Some people have said we are here simply to participate in the development of the human race. Many others have thrown up their hands and proclaimed life meaningless, and they pursue the question no further. A religious view pushes us onward to seek more meaningful alternatives.

"If buying isn't the answer, and waiting on people doesn't always help, and realizing my potential isn't enough, where in the world does that leave me?!" Jayne spoke for the group as she summarized the discussion to date.

The women were sensing what had been going on in their lives. Jayne voiced it, "The purposes others lay on me don't seem to 'take,' no matter how much they say the shoulds and oughts." Sue Ann added, "The shoulds and oughts just don't make it with depressed people!" Lori observed that the backlash against the women's movement wasn't really helping. "By saying we're *supposed* to be satisfied with being at home, society just creates another layer of other-people-out-there telling us what to do." Carolyn finally put her finger on the dilemma when she noted " . . . how empty it feels to wake up and discover I've been going through the motions of purpose and roles . . . all ones others have chosen *for* me."

Carolyn and I talked mid-week about the emptiness she was experiencing. We spoke of a deep canyon, an abyss, that had to be faced, and ultimately crossed. For some women the gaping hole in their path swallows them up for a time. Some women experience the abyss as pain. Many more experience it as numbness. Other women go for months, even years, with the problem unacknowledged. The extensive use of Valium and alcohol may well be symptomatic of women's uneasiness with what the culture offers as reasons for living.

"Beware of fearing the yawning hole so much that you dare not face the questions," I told the group the next time we met. I suggested that those who dare to fall deeply are lifted by "updrafts" of the Spirit and usually find the firmest ground on the other side. The key to finding your way to the other side is admitting that the having and the doing aren't working. The key is in letting go.

Letting Go

Jayne began sharing her fear of the bottomless canyon that her questions were leading her into. "I've reached a point of all or nothing. I can only walk on the other side of the canyon when I really leave behind all that's on the first side."

"But doesn't this idea of letting go contradict what you taught us about taking charge?" Gwen challenged. Yes, it does. But frequently the most profound aspects of life are paradoxical; two things that seem to be opposite are both true. I emphasized that while it is essential for women to take charge of their lives and to take responsibility for getting themselves out of depression, it's also just as crucial that, at some point, they let go of all they've held onto too tightly, in order to let the future come to them.

I shared with the group the story *Hope for the Flowers*. Trina Paulus describes caterpillars living the pleasant life of munching leaves and crawling around with other caterpillars. Eventually the caterpillar life proves to be unsatisfying, having no real point to it. Climbing caterpillar pillars proves pointless—there's nothing to be found at the top. Then comes the vision, the possibility of living on a whole different level, to be able to fly . . . as a butterfly. But one can get there only by dying to all of what caterpillar-ness means. The risk must be taken: roll up in a cocoon, never knowing for sure if you'll come out on the other side or just die in there. The reward for taking the risk is to fly instead of crawl.

How to Find the Other Side

What are some practical steps to finding a new purpose? What specific things can you do from day to day to discover what is satisfying and meaningful for you? How do you find footing on the other side?

Your journal continues to be a faithful friend. You can review the entries you made while you worked through Chapter 8 on gifts and life planning. Most women find their purpose by looking in the direction of their gifts and who they are, uniquely, as a person. Before then, though, your journal is a place to spell out what is empty about your life. Describe on paper what is dissatisfying, and try to probe the possible reasons why. Ask lots of questions of yourself, of the situation you find yourself in, of the larger world. Speculate about the meanings you find around you. Write out the possibilities you discover, the thoughts and inklings that cross your mind. Reread earlier entries and reflect on what you find. Record your new reactions to old experiences.

Reading forms a vital part of discovery. People through the ages have struggled with the purpose question. Delve into their works and see if they have found some of what you are looking for. As you read, record in your journal the thoughts and questions you find most helpful. Hold a conversation with a book.

Another way to get at the questions of purpose is to begin asking your friends, "What do *you* think (or feel) life is all about?" Many people will not have thought about it at all in those terms. A few will have illuminating insights.

Conversations about purpose in your small group will be particularly valuable. These few friends may well be, among everyone you know, the only people as vitally interested in these great questions as you are. Take full advantage of the energy and enthusiasm while you have it. The group is a place to test out new hunches and verbalize possibilities to see if indeed they make any sense. If your discoveries seem to be leading you against the tide of the culture around you, the group can provide valuable support in your quest.

Nancy had no medical training, yet because of her medical history she found herself almost overnight in the position of informing doctors and nurses about the implications in caring for patients with lung disease. For her, too, the self-doubts flooded in. Sue Ann said to Nancy, "Of course you don't know everything. But neither do those doctors. Just don't forget you've been somewhere they haven't. You have a story to tell."

The process of finding a purpose in your life is just that, a process. It evolves over time, and it happens differently for each one of us. For most it is a gradual dawning, as pieces begin to fit together in a jigsaw puzzle and the picture gradually becomes distinguishable. As with the puzzle on the game-room table, life goes on while we now and then stop by the table and fit a few more pieces in. Your answers will always be partial.

Suggested Assignments

1. Try to analyze what the present culture is telling you your purpose in life should be. Examine advertising, family ideas and tradition, your church's teaching, for example. Then list your own ideas, and ask several friends for their responses. How do you feel about the purposes others are suggesting?

2. Ask yourself the following questions, then "interview" several people who share your life situation using the same questions. What do you like best about what you do? What do you get a kick out of? What *feels* most important? What seems like it must *be* most important? What in your life would you not want anyone to take away from you? People? Why? Things you do? Why? Church? Beliefs? Roles? Securities? Why?

    Reflect in your journal on what seems most purposeful in life *for you*. Share with one other person what you learned from doing this.

3. Consider these two hypothetical situations: If you somehow knew your entire region would be flooded tomorrow and everything familiar would be washed away, what would you most want to hang onto? What would be your role in or relationship with that person/place/thing/group? Why is it important to you?

    If you knew you had just one year to live and you'd not be debilitated during that time with illness, what would you want to be sure to be or do? Why is this important?

4. What would be your response if a person came up to you and sincerely asked, "Why do you think you are alive?" Answer this in writing *after* you've done all the above exercises. Has your thinking been changed by this process?

5. If you are interested in possible spiritual answers to your life-purpose questions, read Chapter 11.

Suggested Readings

Viktor Frankl, *Man's Search for Meaning*. New York: Simon & Schuster, Pocket Books, 1976. This is a classic on the question of our purpose in life.

Trina Paulus, *Hope for the Flowers*. New York: Paulist Press, 1972.

John Kenneth Galbraith, *Economics and the Public Purpose*. New York: Signet, 1973. Chapter 4, "Consumption and the Concept of the Household," discusses women as "managers of consumption."

Colette Dowling, *Cinderella Complex*. New York: Pocket Books, 1982. One woman's struggle with dependency.

Reading biographies is another fine way to get in touch with one's purpose in life. Your local college or library probably lists famous and less well-known women under "Women's Studies." Guaranteed to inspire.

11

Integrating Faith with Life

I address the thoughts and convictions in this chapter to several different types of readers: to those who are not religious at all but may be curious to see what I have to say; to those who consider themselves faithful or spiritual but have no interest in or connection with the organized church; and to those who are church members but have not yet figured out how their faith or their understanding of God relate to overcoming depression.

For all these readers I write the following out of my own belief that getting connected with God "makes all the difference" in life. I base my own life and work on the assumption that life is lived best when we are "attuned" to our Creator. For me that attunement happens best through Jesus. Because I consider the spiritual approach essential to overcoming depression, I therefore offer the following discussions: prayer as a way of life (an extension of Chapter 4), prayer and our self-image (Chapter 7), giftedness (Chapter 8), and taking charge and letting go (Chapters 9 and 10).

Prayer as a Way of Life

In a workshop on prayer I once asked the group to think up images for how they imagined prayer worked or how they practiced it. One person explained that she prayed as if God worked like the telephone system, where the circuits ring "busy" if too many calls come in at once. She tried carefully, she said, to pray only for "the important things" so as not to tie up the lines with "trivial matters." Another person said she prayed like a lawyer arguing at a trial, trying to convince God—the judge—of either her innocence or of her right to a certain material reward. A third person admitted she felt like a junior high student in her first public speaking class. She felt she could never find the right words, and so she never ventured to try unless she was called upon. Nearly everyone acknowledged they turned to God in crises, hoping he would bail them out.

For the woman caught in mild depression, prayer must be bigger than her old images. For prayer to become a stimulus to personal change, it must become a process in which she begins to open her entire self to the reality of God.

Several months after that same workshop, I checked back with the participants to see if their understanding of prayer had changed. One person commented, "The scariest part about praying is knowing at the outset that I must be willing to change and *be changed* by God."

Learning to pray means "growing up" as a praying person, for prayer implies some good news and some bad news. The bad news is that prayer is probably more often *our* accepting what God wants than God's coming around to what *we* want. The good news is that what God wants is better for us than what we've thought up. One woman summed up her new insights about prayer this way: "I'm learning to get out of my own way and into God's way."

Sometimes the most difficult step for us is to be willing to be part of the answer to our own prayers, to be open to all kinds of new possibilities. This often means being willing to take more responsibility for our lives in conjunction with God's direction. I like to call the process "getting in phase with God's purpose" or "centering."

Another workshop participant said, "Now I see it as a real *conversation* with God. Sometimes I get to talk; sometimes I must listen. The listening is the most exciting time because it always means some transformation in me." "Listening" in prayer is first becoming attuned to hearing that still, small voice inside us. But it is also becoming sensitive to other voices. As a depressed person grows less preoccupied with her own problems, she becomes more able to hear other messages. A sermon is one obvious voice. Would you "hear," for example, a sermon on Jesus healing a paralytic? Could you acknowledge that you, too, are paralyzed? Would you be able to say, "Yes, I am a victim of my moods, often trapped like the man who lived on a stretcher"? If a sermon or anyone's remarks set off these thoughts, would you be able to hear them for what they are and then allow them to change you? Would you be moved to action or decision? Or would you remain apathetic and defensive?

In *Clarity in Prayer,* David Jacobsen has suggested the idea of telling God the "small 't' truth" about our lives in prayer. This approach to prayer brings great clarity. It is also an excellent depression fighter. As suggested earlier, confusion and fuzziness are often at the core of depression. Clarity about what is real, what you want, what God wants, all work to lift the fog of depression. Telling the small "t" truth (Jacobsen contrasts it to the great Truths about which we can really say very little for certain) can mean many things. It means telling God what's going on in your life. You can do it in your mind, in your journal, or out loud. "Well, God, today I really feel. . . ." The Spirit of God finds a channel into us when we tell the truth from our own point of view, and *this* is empowering!

Prayer can transform the methods of behavior modification described in Chapter 4. Where behavior modification is essentially talking to ourselves, prayer is talking with One who is infinitely greater than we are. Prayer is tapping into the ultimate source of power and of wisdom, asking God to change us. Prayer allows us to reach a level never possible through even the best of psychological alternatives alone. We need them all working together.

Prayer and Our Self-Image

In Chapter 7 we discussed ways to improve self-image. Christian women sometimes have a special problem with self-image. I often hear questions such as, "Doesn't God want us to be humble?" Many Christian women I have talked to worry about becoming too conceited or self-satisfied when they hear me encouraging positive self-image building.

The problem with the put-yourself-down-in-the-name-of-humility tradition (for that's what often happens) is that it's bad theology. Somewhere along the line people came up with the idea that humility means thinking we're not very good. While it's central to Christian belief that we all sin—and that's why Christ had to come in order to reconcile us with God—it's paradoxically true that we must learn to love ourselves, just as God loves us.

The Gospel has as one of its central themes the concise text: "Love your neighbor as yourself." Most people read this to mean, "Love your neighbor a lot," or "Love your neighbor as much as you imagine other people love themselves." Few see that they'll need to learn to love themselves much more in order to love their neighbor as much as God intends. Loving your neighbor (at the heart of God's message) involves developing a healthy self-image, a sound self-love, a generous self-confidence. Loving your neighbor depends on it!

Look at what God does in the Bible. He appoints everyday people to do what he thinks needs doing. He appoints Moses to free his people from slavery. Moses has a low self-image, "Oh no, not me. I'd be no good at that." God listens to no such excuses. Moses' "humility" almost interferes with getting the job done.

Jesus, by contrast, is the "five-star" example of calm self-assurance. And God's act of sending Jesus underscores how valuable we are, how much we are "worth it." God expects us to carry on the work Jesus was doing: healing people, putting their lives back together, showing them God loves them. There is no place for false humility here. I do not believe self put-downs and denials of gifts are the kind of "humility" God expects of us. Rather, we are to take reasoned stock of ourselves and our gifts with sober judgment and thankfulness.

Prayer can help us with self-image by getting us to listen to God and his guidance instead of maintaining our inaccurate self-dislike; by helping us to discern the path most nearly in the direction God is going; by allowing a glimpse of a wholly new horizon, or getting in on something far bigger than ourselves, or growing step by step, day by day, into the full persons God intends us to be.

We have noted that listening is a part of prayer frequently overlooked. Try listening to your journal and what it can reveal to you about yourself. Listen to the Bible as you let yourself read it freshly. Listen to others around you and in your group when they compliment you even though you don't believe it, or when they're concerned about you and you don't feel you deserve all that attention. God knows you're worth it! In all these ways, and many more, God's Spirit may be trying to get through to you what a magnificent person you really are.

Ask God to teach you the full meaning of his love for you. It may well be a lifetime project for you to realize God is for you. God is on your side, at your side. Your Creator wants the best for you. If we could actually catch a glimpse of how much God loves each one of us, we'd be on top of the world, incredibly energized by a refreshing self-confidence, because of the confidence God has in us.

Giftedness as a Way of Life

Self-image and a recognition of our giftedness are intertwined. Our gifts are not some alien qualities imposed on us, foreign to our nature; they *are us,* part of who we are as unique persons. Despite this truth, a particular form of self-put-down is common today among some very devout Christians. You can recognize it in such statements as, "Don't give me any credit; the Lord did it all." Or, "I couldn't have done that myself; it was the Lord's power entirely." While it's quite true that God does indeed empower us far beyond what we might have mustered ourselves, the heresy lies in the way we belittle ourselves in the process. Too often we imagine that we, the very creation of God's hands, are worth nothing. But surely God would not have planned for us to do Christ's work if we were feeble creatures or mere "tools." He chose us to *be* his hands on earth; and to that end he has equipped us with a multitude of talents and energies and the potential to accomplish all the good work he wants done.

The subject of using our gifts and abilities came up one day when our original group was discussing John Holland's careers material. Lori asked, "Does any of this have anything to do with being a Christian?" "It certainly does," I answered. The Apostle Paul was onto what John Holland much later discovered, but Paul used different terms.

"In each of us the Spirit is manifested in one particular way, for some useful purpose. There are varieties of gifts, but the same Spirit" (1 Cor. 12:7,4).

Paul speaks at length to the Christians at Corinth and at Rome about the gifts and abilities they have received from God and the proper use of them. He leaves no doubt that these gifts are intended to be used to their fullest. Just as with Jesus' parable of the talents, Paul's words make it clear that to fail to use the gifts God gives not only cheats the community but wastes the life of the person to whom the talents are given.

Paul's lists of gifts are not the same as Holland's six categories. Clearly their purposes are different. But their insight is the same: People don't match; they are very different and are called to different tasks, different roles. Paul's lists of gifts are not meant to be complete, but merely illustrative of the types of abilities God is interested in and sees as necessary for the overall task of building up the Body of Christ, the Church. Paul mentions among others the gifts of inspired utterance or prophecy, administration, teaching, stirring speech, giving of money or goods, leadership, helping others; he also mentions wisdom, knowledge, faith, healing, miraculous powers, the ability to interpret tongues; he lists as possessors of these gifts apostles, evangelists, "shepherds," and teachers. A quick glance at this list reveals abilities ranging far beyond the traditional twentieth-century housewives' role. Clearly God intends for women to find themselves all along the spectrum.

God gives each one of us the talents required to do our unique part in contributing to God's work in our corner of the world. The genius of this theology of gifts is illustrated in the parts-of-the-body metaphor that Paul suggests. One person may function as a toe, another as a kidney, a third as an elbow or a kneecap. Paul mocks the idea that we should all function as the same parts—all as mouths or all as hands. The conformity our current culture tries to impose would make us all eyes or all ears. Imagine the distorted body if there were not a rich variety of functions and abilities. Paul encourages relishing the diversity God has created.

Paul and Holland address the same reality from different vantage points. Gifts and talents are to be used to their fullest; doing so is much of what life is about. Both writers realize that people come in very different packages, that people have wide-ranging abilities that will be used in widely and gloriously different situations. Life is lived at its best when each person can cluster her activities around her unique grouping of interests, gifts, and talents.

What does this theology mean for the depressed housewife? It means you have a God-given uniqueness waiting to be developed. It means you can move off center into a more fulfilling, rewarding, and satisfying life, doing the special things God has equipped you to do. It's tremendously energizing to be a specialist for God's cause! Feeling unique and valuable is an unequalled antidote for the greyness of depression.

Taking Charge and Letting Go as a Paradoxical but Possible Way of Life

The strong position on personal responsibility I take in Chapter 9 makes some Christian women uneasy. One said to me, "Doesn't what you're saying take away from our dependence on God? Aren't you calling for something which pulls us away from our proper reliance on God in our lives?" I knew the answer was no, but it takes some reflection to help someone understand why. I suggested she begin by asking herself exactly what God wanted her to do if she *didn't* take responsibility for her life.

Somehow a misconception has developed that confuses *dependence* on God with *trust*. People think of God as provider, comforter, guide, and sustainer of life. But "dependence" implies a certain helplessness that simply is not characteristic of truly adult human beings. There is a difference between being dependent on God, as an infant is dependent on its parents, and trusting God with one's life. Unfortunately, this dependent mindset slips over too easily into human relationships. Women find themselves feeling dependent on husbands and other primary persons instead of trusting them in relationships of interdependence. Rather than take responsibility for their own lives and feelings, these women defer all responsibility to these other persons.

Two popular beliefs have contributed to the confusion between dependence and trust. The first comes from a phrase often misattributed to the Bible: "God helps those who help themselves." Ben Franklin authored this, and it means that you should pretty much ignore God and go your own way, doing the very best you can on your own strength. God may throw in a few goodies now and then, but don't count on it. This bootstrap approach by itself has not proved particularly helpful to depressed women.

The "well-sharpened instrument" approach holds that we are just God's tools, used by him to do his will on earth. While it is certainly true that God depends on people to achieve his ends among us, the difficulty with this philosophy is its assumption that God bypasses the gifts and talents, resources and abilities he has given us. To view ourselves as mindless tools insults both our integrity and his judgment. It also provides us with an excuse for not taking responsibility for our lives. We, as women, can lapse into a mindless servitude under the delusion that this is what God expects of us. He expects far more! And he has equipped us to become far more.

It takes nothing away from God to see him as ultimately trustworthy and yourself as equipped to manage quite well. This shift in your view allows your trust in him to mature and it becomes both a reflection and a nurturer of your trust in yourself. What a delight to begin to see yourself as a trustworthy person! You can rely on yourself to come through in a difficult situation. You move into each day with a calm confidence about your place in God's world. And as your self-confidence grows, your ability to reach out expands. You open yourself up to life as you find you can trust others at deeper and deeper levels.

As your personal power develops, your power over depression also increases. Circumstances that used to pull you down

are now subject to your positive action. You begin to understand what it means to ask the question, "If God is with me,
who can be against me?"

While we are learning to take charge of our lives, we are
also called to the single most difficult and rewarding step of
our lives. The question is: "Shall I control my life as I see fit
or shall I attune to God's way and relinquish my stubbornness
to his wisdom?" This surrender is the ultimate spiritual bridge
to be crossed.

The Christian concept of achieving resurrection through death
is a scary one. In *Hope for the Flowers* the caterpillar cannot
know when she enters the cocoon whether she'll ever come
out alive. But she chooses to relinquish her caterpillar-ness to
become God's butterfly. Nicodemus learned that he had to be
born again in order to enter God's Kingdom. In the Garden
of Gethsemane Jesus had to repeat three times, "Father, not
my will, but thine be done." (I believe he said it three times
in order to really mean it.) Letting go and free-falling into
God's embrace to find his purpose for our lives is our greatest
and most promising calling and test. Letting go is *essential*
when we're searching for purpose in life.

Henri Nouwen helps us understand the kind of prayer that
helps us learn to let go. In his book *With Open Hands* he
speaks of prayers of longing and prayers of hope. "The prayer
of little faith is where you hold fast to the concrete of the
present situation in order to win a certain security. . . . The
concreteness of the wishes . . . eliminates the possibility for
hope" (Ave Maria Press, 1978, p. 80). He speaks of persons
of little faith closing themselves off from what might be coming
by demanding only certain answers. Prayers of hope, by contrast, ultimately trust the Giver and trusting the Giver with our
lives can bring the deepest purpose of all. Hope dares to stay
open to whatever the day, the month, the year will offer. Hope
allows no room for depression.

Paul's letter to the Christians in Rome sets out another clear
signpost for identifying our purpose in life as it relates to letting
go. He speaks of what we are ultimately to do with our lives.
He begins the twelfth chapter with the word "therefore." He

means, because of what I've said so far . . . because you are free, my brothers and sisters, because you are no longer bound up by the law, no longer in the cage of impossible expectations, because through what Christ has done, you no longer need to try to live up to all those myths of perfection. . . . Therefore, you are free to make a *choice* about your life. Because you've been given life as a gift, you are free to give it back to God.

Paul recalls the Old Testament imagery of sacrificing animals on the altar but adds a paradoxical twist: "Offer your very selves to him: a *living* sacrifice. . . ." Give yourself over to God's purpose, but stay alive to do it. It's not the end as it is for sacrificed animals; it's just the beginning of life for you. In *The New Testament in Modern English*, J. B. Phillips translates the second verse of the twelfth chapter (Romans) brilliantly: "Don't let the world around you squeeze you into its own mold." Once you've offered yourself to God, dead to the old ways and purposes, don't let them suck you back in. Don't live on the new side of the canyon as if you were still back on the old side. Don't crawl around when you have new yellow wings.

How are you to do this? By sheer willpower? We all know that doesn't work for long. "Be transformed. . . ." The verb is passive. God does the transforming, if you allow him. "Be transformed by the renewal of your mind. . . ." You can take on a whole new way of thinking, a whole new way of perceiving your world, a whole new outlook.

"Then you will be able to discern the will of God, and to know what is good, acceptable, and perfect" (Rom. 12:2). In discussing their sought-after purpose in life, people may ask, "How can I know God's will for my life?" Paul has unobtrusively slipped a major clue into these two verses: If you want to find out God's will for your life, avoid being conformed to this world's will for you. Offer yourself, your life, to God and you'll begin to discover the answer.

In the end, breaking through means letting God break through into your life. When that sunlight floods in, depression is crowded out and a more purpose-full life begins.

Suggested Readings

Henri J. M. Nouwen, *With Open Hands*. Notre Dame, Ind.: Ave Maria Press, 1978. The finest book I've seen on letting go.

Robert C. Leslie, *Jesus and Logotherapy*. Nashville: Abingdon, 1965. An interesting exploration of the meaning question in the New Testament.

David Jacobsen, *Clarity in Prayer: Telling the small 't' truth*. Corte Madera, Calif.: Omega Books, 1976. (Available from the author, 60 Park Ave., Mill Valley, Calif., 94941.) Also check your local Christian bookstore for current titles on prayer and devotional subjects. There are many.

PART FOUR

Tips on Support Groups

A

Starting Your Own

Not everyone who reads this book will feel up to starting her own group to work through the material with others. But a good number of housewives who experience depression also experience periods of energy and enthusiasm, or at least times of normal moods. It's during these "up" times that you who feel inclined to start a group can talk to friends about the book and find others who are interested.

The key is to locate just *one* friend who is interested in starting a group. Make a pact that between you you'll make it happen. Agree that you'll rely on the other when one is feeling down. You may both feel discouraged at times; you'll no doubt have your weaker moments. But it's important to "hang in there!" Once you get started, it will be worth it. The other women who join you will thank you over and over for giving them the opportunity for a brighter life.

At your first planning meeting with your friend, begin writing a list of people you both know who might be interested in joining you. Make a point to talk about your idea at the other places you find yourself . . . friends at the market, a neighbor you run into at the cleaners. If you feel shy about asking someone to join, try saying, "Helen and I are hoping to start a group to discuss the book *Breaking Through* to help us all get rid of those gray days we all feel now and then. Do you know of anyone who might be interested?" After you've said this a few times, you may get bolder and admit more to the depression you yourself feel. The more open you are about your bad days, the more you free the listener to admit to her feelings on those days when you don't see her. Remember, she truly believes she's the only one who feels that way, and she's not about to admit it *until* she hears you say you feel that way too.

Start a second list of all the likely places you might distribute a brochure about the group: at your church? other churches in the area? good friends who could spread the word for you? clubs you belong to? newsletters of your groups? PTA? school newsletter? a community school for adult enrichment? Also call your local community college. They probably have women's studies classes, and those instructors may be willing to pass on your brochures. The counseling staff there no doubt knows of women who are likely candidates. Tell them what you're doing, and leave a stack of brochures. When you begin to feel more bold, call up a reporter from the feature section of your local paper (it used to be called the women's pages; now perhaps it's "People"). See if she or he would like to do a short story on you and your friends as initiators of a self-help group. One warning: You may get more calls than you can take. You may find people coming to you from everywhere. Be thinking about who else in your community might be interested in facilitating a second group.

Decide on a place to meet. It's a good idea to have one place for all ten weeks. The living room atmosphere is best. People feel most comfortable about sharing their personal lives in a warm setting. If you must use an institutional setting, a church lounge with carpet and softly upholstered furniture is next best (not vinyl couches and green linoleum, if you can avoid it!). Better to be squeezed intimately into a cozy living room than rattling around in an echoing social hall.

Someone may suggest that you switch around to homes of the group members once you get started. It's not forbidden, but here are a couple of reasons not to encourage it: Every now and then someone will be inclined to miss a week. If she's not sure where the new house is, and she's feeling low and unadventurous anyway, she may quite likely just skip it and stay home. Secondly, several in your group may have the housework blahs and not want anyone to see their living room. If some want to have the group at their homes, it can put unnecessary pressure on others who do not and who feel uncomfortable saying no.

The ideal place is the home of one of you who start the group. If this won't work, perhaps you can find a third friend with a suitable house. There should be no obligation for the hostess to provide food or beverages, after the first time. The group will decide if they want to sip or nibble and should take turns bringing goodies.

Next, decide on a time to meet. You should allow a minimum of two hours. A little longer is better. A period of about two and a half hours satisfies most group members.

Get out your calendar and block out the ten weeks, once you have decided on which day of the week you prefer. Check for possible holidays and school vacation days that would disrupt your meetings. Then draw up a checklist including the following items and check them off as you determine or take care of them: place, time, dates, cost, books ordered, brochures printed, brochures distributed, notebooks purchased.

Cost is the next item you must decide on. Obviously, you want to keep it as low as possible, so no one is excluded simply for economic reasons. Here's what you'll want to consider:

1. It gives a nice psychological boost to the women to receive a colorful three-ring notebook in the beginning of the class. Check large variety stores or school/office departments for a wide selection of floral prints and inspiring life-lovers like Snoopy. August is a good time to get bargain prices. The notebook (include twenty-five sheets of lined paper) helps each woman feel she's actually enrolled in a *class,* an actual entity which meets every week, does homework, and reports on progress. The gentle reinforcement and encouragement of book and notebook are very important at the beginning.

2. Order this book from your local bookseller in advance. If their local warehouse doesn't stock it, you'll need to allow six to eight weeks. If you do the ordering *first,* you should have them in time for the first class meeting. You may be panicking right now. "What if the people don't come and I am the proud owner of ten books?" First of all, with any effort at all on your part, the group *will* happen. Second, if disaster strikes, you'll be surprised how easily you can tell people what you've learned by reading, explain your dilemma, and they'll gladly buy one from you. You may need to make an advance

deposit on your order. (You'll have to play banker until you collect registration fees. That's one reason it's nice to have a colleague to help share the load.) If one or two arrive the first week with their own books, just tell the class. They'll each have a neighbor or a sister-in-law who "really needs it" and they'll probably buy your extras as gifts. A final suggestion: Your bookseller may let you take copies on consignment; it's worth asking.

3. People may want to bring tea bags, fruit juice, coffee cake, or apples. But you might want to build into the registration fee a small sum for the hostess to provide the hot beverages each week. Use your own judgment.

4. You may from time to time come across articles or work sheets that you'd like everyone to have. If you add a small duplicating fee to the budget, you'll be able to do this. Or, you can simply show people the articles and copy them for whoever is willing to hand you the dimes on the spot. I prefer the built-in charge; it's simpler.

Once you've totalled up your estimates of the above four items, consider whether the people in the neighborhood, church, or area you'll be drawing from will be able to pay this. Remember, you'll be meeting for ten weeks (two and a half months). You might compare it to the fee for a two-credit course at your local community college to see if you're in the ballpark. You can mention the comparison when people call and question the fee.

A final word on cost. It's a well known, if perhaps unfortunate, fact that people value things in our society for what they're worth monetarily. We tend to be more diligent in attending a class that charges a small fee than we would be for a free one. This small investment works as an added incentive on those gray and dubious days when each woman wonders if she really wants to get out of the house and come to the group.

Now you're ready to plan the layout of your brochure. A sample appears on pp. 183-85. You have several alternatives: photocopy the sample as it is, use the sample's design and wording, or create your own. If you choose to photocopy the sample, make a copy of the information on pp. 183-85 on a single side of your brochure so that, when folded in thirds, one column appears within each fold. On the left flap of the reverse side, list a name, address, and telephone number for people to contact for registration. On the right flap of the reverse side, copy this book's cover. The middle column should have space for a mailing label (or address) and stamp. Then find a local printing shop or a large photocopy machine to make your copies, depending on how much you want to pay. At this writing, 100 copies (2 sides) of 8 1/2" X 14" cost about $10.00 on standard paper. Check, however, for heavier paper. For an additional $2.50 you can choose a brighter color (I like canary yellow or vivid orange) and heavier stock, giving your brochure, and your group, a more substantial image. Include this printing or photocopying cost when you calculate the course fee. Allow time to fold the brochures after you pick them up, or pay extra for the shop to do it.

Plan a generous lead time. You should distribute your brochures about four weeks before the announced date of the first class. It takes time for word to get around. If you can arrange it, your newspaper feature story should appear about ten days before the starting date. (Your paper may have other ideas, so inquire.) Have one or two phone numbers on the brochure for people to call with their questions. Answer inquiries cheerfully and enthusiastically. Remember, it probably took a lot of courage for that person to take the initiative to call.

It is essential that everyone understands from the outset that this is a *self-help group*. There will be no trained counselors or psychotherapists present, so, as the group's organizer, you should be prepared to do a certain amount of *screening*. It is very important that people whose problems are severe enough to require one-to-one help from a professional are encouraged to seek that help. The primary reason for this rule is that the person needs that highly trained guidance. The second reason, for the benefit of the group as a whole, is that the group must not get bogged down week after week with the overwhelming problems of one member. While you will be of invaluable support and encouragement to each other, no one of you should dominate the group to the exclusion of others who miss the opportunity to share their experiences.

How, you're wondering, will you know if someone has serious depression. When they call to inquire, ask them why they are particularly interested in taking the course or joining the group. You may find yourself hearing many life stories. If you've already read the first chapter of this book, you'll have a feel for the kind of depression we're talking about. If, for example, someone says they are also going to group therapy on Thursdays, or to their analyst on Wednesdays, you can suggest they stick with that, rather than confuse the two kinds of treatments. It is also prudent to avoid dealing with alcoholic women. Alcoholism is an illness in its own right and needs treatment specific to it. Again, you and your group members will not be sufficiently equipped to deal with those kinds of problems. Clearly, you will have to use your own good judgment.

A word of encouragement should be said before you fear you are taking on too much responsibility. We live in an age of experts. We no longer heal our children; we drive them to the doctor for throat cultures. We make or grow little of our own food; it's ready at the supermarket. We don't always teach our children about sex, or morality, or even God. A trained specialist can be relied upon to do these things for us. We may be reaching the time when we will simply have to find ways to take more responsibility for our own lives. It's not that the experts don't know or shouldn't be consulted. The issue is that we must fight the feeling that we are helpless to care for ourselves. We need not feel powerless in the face of experts when it comes to the mild depression that so many of us experience. Have the wisdom to discern when professional help is, indeed, called for. But for the rest of the time, move boldly forward to work at healing yourself and your sisters by mutual caring.

How many persons should you have in the group? Eight makes a good discussion; ten is better to allow for absentees. Twelve is permissible, but it should be the maximum number. With more than twelve, people feel less free to share who they are, and there's not time for everyone to talk each week.

When people phone to inquire and to register, emphasize the commitment each member will be making. Once she decides to join the group (perhaps after the first meeting), she'll make every effort to come every time. The group process cannot work well with drop-ins. And the class does little good for a woman's depression if she stays home whenever she needs the group most!

To register a person who calls and is interested, take her name, address, and phone number, and make sure she knows how to find the meeting place the first week. Confirm the fee; make arrangements for checks or cash to be paid at the end of the first meeting. Tell her when the books will be available. (If they're available before the first meeting, people may want to pay the fee in advance and begin reading.)

Close your conversation with a cheerful and encouraging word to the caller. Make sure she knows how excited you are about the group and how much you're looking forward to getting to know *her*.

BELIEVE IT OR NOT...
A *VERY* COMMON PROBLEM

Nearly every woman at home today experiences occasional or chronic depression. Most of us hide this from the outside world. We see each other when we're at our best!

We feel we are alone in our discouragement, lack of purpose, sensation of being bogged down in life, or inability to find fulfillment in our current situation. Or we may feel tired too much of the time, long for a really close friend, or wish we were really *good* at something.

The list is long, but at the center is a dissatisfaction with our life the way it is, often coupled with a feeling of helplessness to do much about it.

AN UNUSUAL ANSWER

''Breaking Through'' is a rare opportunity to bring significant change to your life.

In a relaxed small-group setting, 10 to 12 women will meet weekly to share concerns, support one another, and learn new possibilities.

A SIGNIFICANT COMMITMENT FOR SIGNIFICANT CHANGE

Change that is important and lasting does not occur overnight. The women who find they are willing to work together for change will "contract" with each other and the leader to a ten-week learning/growing process. A willingness to grow is important; past background is not.

The group will meet:

(Time) _____

At: _____

(Address) _____

YOU WILL EXPERIENCE
AND LEARN ABOUT:

- Self-image building: discover what a super person you are

- Gifts: learn and develop your own gifts and talents

- The medical/physical angle: how hormones and even color may affect your attitudes

- A new look at feminism from an angle that may surprise and even inspire you!

- Lots and lots of specific methods, tools, and ways to change your behavior and attitude to help you become the person you want to be

- An extensive reading list for those who seek more depth

- A diverse and extensive curriculum, yet one that will be flexible enough to deal with the priorities of group members

B

How to Lead One

Long before the first meeting, you may wonder, "How will I lead the group? I'm not a teacher." If so, it's time to redraw your image of what a teacher or a group leader is and does.

There are several philosophies of "leadership." Let's begin by describing several models of leadership you're familiar with to show you what you do *not* need to be. The first model is the college professor who is an authority in his field. People come and "sit at his feet" and he tells them The Truth. On Sesame Street Ernie calls this person the Royal Smart Person. There is a place for such teachers, but a self-help group is not that place.

A more recent model in small groups is the highly trained facilitator. She has all the right words at just the right time to draw everyone out and mold the perfect discussion. Everyone shares openly from the first day, and much growth goes on. This is an effective format, but it does rely heavily on the expertise of the leader. Again, the group members are at the mercy of one person's skills.

A third style is the volunteer discussion leader. You may have met one at an adult study group. The style includes one person who feels comfortable (or at least willing) to see to it that the discussion keeps moving and that each person has a chance to contribute. With this model, we move closer to what your role will be, but in this instance, the other group members sit back until it's their turn, and they rely on the leader to keep the ball rolling.

The fourth model is the one recommended for your new group: shared leadership. Leadership is actually a function, not a role. While one person does need to be the acknowledged coordinator or facilitator (you or your colleague), each person in the group publicly acknowledges that she is willing to help take responsibility for the welfare of the group. This means, for example, that if someone is too cold, she will discreetly get up and close the door, ask the hostess to turn up the heat, or simply put on a coat. If several others notice her initiative, one may interrupt and ask if anyone else is uncomfortable. Adjustments are made and the meeting continues. A second example: Marilyn has been up most of the night with a sick child. She feels herself dozing off, in spite of her interest in the subject. She feels free to simply get up and get herself a cup of coffee without disturbing the person speaking; or she may choose to simply stand while she listens. Everyone understands that these are not interruptions, but merely people taking responsibility for their own learning.

A third example of shared leadership requires more sensitivity, but is not impossible to learn. Joyce begins to sense that the discussion has moved far afield from the intended topic. She is anxious to get back to the point. Instead of waiting for the "leader" to fix it, she breaks in at an appropriate pause and says, "I sense we may be wandering from the point. Does anyone else feel this way? If so, can someone restate the question (problem, issue, dilemma) we've been trying to tackle this morning?" The response may be, "No, I think this tangent is important in its own right, because. . . ." Someone else may then say, "Would you (addressing the group) like to stay with this subject a few more minutes? or move back to the original subject now?" A general consensus can usually be reached easily and informally by nodding heads or quick comments, and the discussion proceeds in the direction the group wishes.

There is no feeling of winning or losing. If the group stays with the tangent, Joyce does not feel as if she's been overruled. She simply realizes that others had a slightly different sense of the significance of the discussion. On the other hand, if several others feel the discussion has strayed, they're grateful to her for breaking in.

Each person actively shares in the responsibility for the group's learning, for its being helpful and supportive, and for making the progress that each woman anticipates. True, some will be more verbal than others, particularly at first. Before the first meeting, for example, some of the women may feel awkward about standing around getting acquainted over coffee. But once they get to know one another, they'll be eager to catch up on how their new friends have been doing all week. This interaction becomes more than a casual social time; the catching up is an important part of the group support process. And each person should help mold the atmosphere so that everyone feels comfortable sharing. The rapport will build over the weeks and the shyer women will feel more acceptance as they become better acquainted.

Toward the end of the first meeting, and again perhaps at the third or fourth, the group can discuss their own list of norms and principles they wish to follow as a group. A *norm* is a behavior or attitude that the whole group agrees upon. Writing up a list clarifies for everyone the expectations each one holds. If members draw up a list and then find that they really don't believe an item is important, and no one follows it, they ought to eliminate it. Here is a list of suggestions, but remember, these are not *your* group's norms unless those women agree to them.

1. Arrive promptly at 9:15. The implied value here is "We think catching up over coffee is an important part of our process." Start at 9:30. "We want to get all we can out of each gathering."

2. Close promptly at 11:30. Some have babysitters to pay or school buses to meet. No one wants to have to leave knowing the discussion is just getting interesting.

3. Keep everything said in the room confidential. The rationale here is essential to the success of the group. "We share scary details of our lives so we can learn from each other. We would be uncomfortable here if we knew our life stories were being discussed later with neighbors or even husbands. We may think it doesn't matter if we repeat a story if the person is unknown to the listener, but as a deep commitment to our new sisters, what's said in the group stays in the group for the inner peace of each one here."

4. Share the leadership. Everyone monitors the atmosphere and the subject matter. Anyone is free and, in fact, expected to speak up or take corrective action when she feels it's called for.
5. Give every person the opportunity to speak at least once each week. The assumption here is: "Every person's experiences are valued by us." Your format can encourage this norm.
6. Give every woman the freedom to speak only when she feels she wants to. Saying, "I pass for now" is acceptable. The group is saying, "We care a great deal for you, but we will not pry. We expect you to take responsibility for your own growth."
7. Make it a conscious goal to affirm others. Say out loud, "Good job," or "You've given us courage to try something and not fear failure." After all, failure is not the end, just the beginning of another learning experience.
8. Try to attend every meeting. If members miss only for the most crucial problems or unavoidable conflicts, they are saying: "We care about each other and about what happens at our meetings." If they must miss, they promise to phone some other member or the hostess.

C

Being an Effective Group Member

Everyone who plans to join a support group should read Section B. As I mentioned there, leadership in your group will be a *function* all members perform. Two types of functions that you can perform in your small group are content functions and process functions.

Content functions have to do specifically with *what* is being said. Examples are:

- Seeing that the topic makes sense with the general goals the group has set out
- Finding an illustration that helps the group understand the point
- Helping to clarify what others are trying to express
- Summarizing what has been said so far or tying together two previous points into an overarching principle
- Offering specific information gleaned from the week's readings or asking if anyone else's readings can inform the discussion.

Process functions have to do not with *what* is being said, but *how* it is being said. It relates to the direction and mood of the discussion. Some examples of process functions might be:

- Reflecting the group's feelings or sharing one's own feelings to see if anyone else shares them
- Encouraging another person, helping her to build her self-image
- Being aware of the way the discussion is proceeding (Is everyone getting a chance to speak or is one person dominating?)
- Suggesting a new norm or reminding the group of an old one.

Some in the group will naturally be more aware of persons' feelings; others will be more content oriented. See how you can function best, and become attuned to monitor the group's progress. You will appreciate each other's sensitivities and contributions as you go on.

The conditions you'll want to foster in the group include some of these feelings or attitudes:

- Empathy for the speaker—hearing and, if possible, feeling what she is trying to communicate
- Sincere caring for each person present, communicating warmth toward others whether or not they seem successful
- A mood of acceptance and openness, allowing congruence, that is, allowing what is showing on the outside of a person to be as close as possible to what is going on inside. An atmosphere of both safety and of caring will promote this mood and will discourage the less helpful behavior of making up a good front to impress others, when one's inner self says something else.

Creating a good group atmosphere is not impossibly difficult, but it does require attention and effort. A good group seldom just "happens." At the end of the ten weeks you'll feel satisfied at having contributed to an important cooperative effort.

After reading the list of group norms suggested in Section B, each group member should be prepared to offer changes and additions for your own group's needs.

D

A Suggested Weekly Schedule

First Meeting (date:_____)

9:15   Gather; name tags, coffee/tea. Hand out books and materials.

9:30 to   Introductions. Going around the circle twice, first
11:00   tell your name and what animal (or bird or fish) you feel like today (not why). The second time around, respond to the question, "Why did you decide to come to this group, and what do you hope to get out of it?"

Leader should keep time so that each person will have adequate time to speak; e.g. nine people in one and a half hours would get ten minutes each, maximum.

Leader may wish to take brief notes on what each one hopes to get out of the group. The list can be a good resource for a reality check in five weeks, an evaluation to see if the group is meeting each person's needs and expectations.

11:00 to   Discuss the concept of norms. List on a chalk
11:20   board or butcher paper the norms the group decides on. (Butcher paper with felt-tip markers allows you to save the list and add to it in later weeks.)

11:20   Give assignments and discuss any questions about them.

Read Chapters 1 and 2 in *Breaking Through*. Select the exercises you will discuss next time.

Ask each person to begin keeping track of mood swings, menstrual cycle, shifts in diet, and significant events, so they'll have a sufficient record when you reach Chapter 6.

11:30   Close.

Second Meeting (date: _____)

Introductions will take less time each week, but provide each person time to speak at least once. Go around the circle telling one thing about yourself that does not relate to your husband or children—an interest or hobby or a place you would like to travel to. Fill in any pertinent life facts you didn't tell the first time.

Discuss the assignment. Relate experiences, findings, and results so far regarding Resistance.

Ask if anyone has had previous experience with journals or if anyone has been in a small group or support group before with positive results.

Assignment: Read Chapters 3 and 4 and do the assignments indicated.

Third Meeting (date: _____)

Introductions: Choose a theme to share that you might not know about each other, e.g. an interest or hobby you once had that you'd like to pick up again someday, a favorite book and why, or a secret wish.

Discuss ways of changing. How did the methods in Chapters 3 and 4 work for you? What specific methods do you plan to try for yourself? How can you help each other keep accountable to your goals?

Assignment: Read Chapter 5 and do the assignments. The group may wish to modify these assignments, focusing on one to discuss or adding to them. Ask if people are reading outside books from the recommended list; plan time for them to report briefly what they are learning.

Fourth Meeting (date:_____)

Discuss the factors in your immediate environment that you each discovered may be affecting your depression. This can be a humorous sharing time! Allow time for each person to share one thing she hopes to tackle right away. Encourage spontaneous co-op painting projects, etc.

Assignment: Read Chapter 6 and do assignments. Plan to bring your journal records on physical factors you've observed.

Fifth Meeting (date:_____)

Discuss physical findings and observations. If you want to have a guest speaker, this would be an ideal time to do that. Prepare your questions in advance, and be sure everyone has read the chapter ahead.

Help each other to be accountable to resolutions about diet and exercise. Mutual encouragement in this area is crucial!

Assignment: Read Chapter 7 and do assignments.

Have someone call to see if the tests mentioned at the end of Chapter 8 are available. Bring to next meeting.

Sixth Meeting (date:_____)

Discuss psychological awarenesses. Did anyone learn anything entirely new? What common themes emerge from the group? Do you find any connections between the physical or environmental factors and the psychological? Decide as a group on ways you'll work on self-image.

Assignment: Read Chapter 8 and do the assignments. Hand out test blanks, if available, from those listed at the end of Chapter 8.

Seventh Meeting (date:_____)

Share with the group the story of your life stages, giving particular emphasis to the possibilities that lie ahead in both the near and distant future.

What significance do you see in finding yourself on the hexagon? Does identifying your type help you see things you want to do differently? How much diversity of types is there within the group? What does this tell you?

How might you begin to use discovered gifts and talents? How can you encourage one another?

Assignment: Read Chapter 9 and do assignments.

Eighth Meeting (date:_____)

Discuss as honestly as you dare your feelings about expectations, freedom, and sense of power and powerlessness. Discuss changes you are going to make.

Assignment: Read Chapter 10 and do assignments.

Ninth Meeting (date:_____)

Discuss the social pressures you feel with regard to purpose in life. Then try to articulate to the group your own sense of purpose, as best you can at this point. Do not be concerned that some have a clearer handle on this question than you do. Answers in this area can take years to come.

Assignment: If your group decides to discuss Chapter 11, read it and note any new insights in your journal.

Review what you have learned throughout the course; reread your journal, the chapters, class notes. Prepare a brief written summary of the course for next week's meeting. Highlight what has been most meaningful and growth-producing for you.

Tenth Meeting (date:_____)

Have each person take ten to fifteen minutes (divide time accordingly) to present her key learnings and new patterns—an overview of what has happened to her during the past ten weeks. Also share future hopes and plans.

Optional Eleventh Meeting (date:_____)

Discuss how prayer is or has been important in your own life with regard to depression. Reserve at least half the meeting to discuss the tension between taking charge of your life and letting go to acknowledge God's power.

If individuals have been particularly special to you, be sure to let them know.

Set up pairs for future accountability, if you like.

Some groups plan quarterly luncheons to report successes and failures and simply to renew friendships.

A salad potluck to close this final meeting can add a special touch to celebrate your life together.